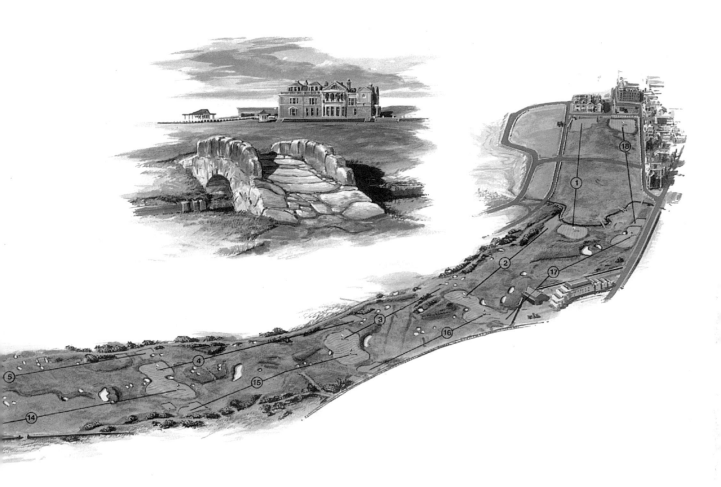

134TH OPEN CHAMPIONSHIP
Card of the Championship Course

Hole	Par	Yards	Hole	Par	Yards
1	4	376	10	4	380
2	4	453	11	3	174
3	4	397	12	4	348
4	4	480	13	4	465
5	5	568	14	5	618
6	4	412	15	4	456
7	4	390	16	4	423
8	3	175	17	4	455
9	4	352	18	4	357
Out	36	3,603	In	36	3,676
			Total	72	7,279

Hazleton Publishing Ltd
5th Floor, Mermaid House, 2 Puddle Dock, London EC4V 3DS
Hazleton Publishing Ltd is a member of Profile Media Group Plc

Published 2005 by Hazleton Publishing Ltd

Copyright © 2005 R&A Championships Limited

Statistics of The 134th Open Championship produced on a
Unisys Computer System

Course map courtesy of The Majors of Golf

Assistance with records provided by Peter Lewis,
Stewart McDougall and Salvatore Johnson

A CIP catalogue record for this book is available
from the British Library

ISBN: 1-903135-49-4

Design and production by Davis Design
Printed in Great Britain

THE OPEN CHAMPIONSHIP

WRITERS
Robert Sommers
Mike Aitken
David Davies
John Hopkins
Lewine Mair
Michael McDonnell

PHOTOGRAPHERS
Getty Images

David Cannon
Richard Heathcote
Ross Kinnaird
Warren Little
Andrew Redington
Jamie Squire

Richard Martin-Roberts
Golf Editor
Steve Rose
Chief Editor

EDITOR
Bev Norwood

The Championship Committee

CHAIRMAN
Martin Kippax

DEPUTY CHAIRMAN
Peter Unsworth

COMMITTEE

Geoffrey Clay	Jim McArthur
John Crawshaw	Lout Mangelaar Meertens
Charles Donald	Richard Muckart
Alan Holmes	Colin Strachan
Rodney James	Nigel Watt

ADVISORY MEMBER
Desmond Duffy
Council of National Golf Unions

CHIEF EXECUTIVE
Peter Dawson

DIRECTOR OF CHAMPIONSHIPS
David Hill

DIRECTOR OF RULES AND EQUIPMENT STANDARDS
David Rickman

The R&A is golf's world rules and development body and organiser of The Open Championship. It operates with the consent of more than 125 national and international, amateur and professional organisations, from over 110 countries and on behalf of an estimated 28 million golfers in Europe, Africa, Asia-Pacific and The Americas (outside the USA and Mexico). The United States Golf Association (USGA) is the game's governing body in the United States and Mexico.

Introduction

By Martin Kippax
Chairman of Championship Committee
The R&A

A St Andrews Open is always extra special and so it proved to be on the occasion of The 134th Open Championship this year.

Jack Nicklaus, arguably the finest golfer ever to strike a ball, chose the Home of Golf to finish his illustrious career. The winner of 18 major championships, and no worse than third in a further 25 Majors, bid a tearful farewell to St Andrews. The rapturous applause and the esteem in which this greatest of Champions is held meant hardly a dry eye in the house.

The wonderful weather enabled Gordon Moir and Euan Grant to weave their own magic in the preparation of the golf course.

The Old Course, despite some doubters, proved the winner in the end with only one player, the eventual Champion, achieving better than 10 under par over the four days' play. Scottish interest was feverish with Colin Montgomerie putting in the strongest of performances to finish runner-up, with two fine Scottish amateurs also faring well. Lloyd Saltman, 19 years of age, won the Silver Medal with a score of 283, with Eric Ramsay only one shot behind.

Tiger Woods was at his imperial best, winning with a score of 274. The excellence and consistency of his game over the four days could not be rivalled. The Old Course is his favourite and his win was fully deserved.

I must thank the St Andrews Championship Committee who, with their staff, worked tirelessly to ensure the presentation of the Old Course in the most excellent condition. Similarly, we are indebted to the hundreds of volunteers for their enthusiastic assistance in running The Open.

Martin Kippax

Foreword

By Tiger Woods

I fell in love with the Old Course at St Andrews the first time I played it as an amateur in 1995, which I still remember so well, playing every one of the 18 holes into the wind and thinking, "What a great golf course!"

Then before this year's final round, I had one of the best warm-up sessions I've ever had. I was hitting the ball so well. I wanted to carry that warm-up session to the course, and I was able to do that. It was one of those rounds I will be thinking about for a long time. I am very thankful it happened at the right time.

This was a week I thought a lot about my father, who was not well enough to come to St Andrews. He was at home, fighting, as always, being stubborn. I was thinking if my father can grind through what he is going through, then I certainly can do this. I'm trying to do everything to make him be as positive as he can be. I can't wait to give him a hug, and to see his face when I hand him the Claret Jug again.

I completed my first career Grand Slam here five years ago, and now to have completed a second career Grand Slam here, at the home of golf, is very special. It is something you dream about. All players want to win The Open Championship, and especially to win at St Andrews. It doesn't get any sweeter than this.

It was also special to be here on the week when Jack Nicklaus brought his career in The Open Championship to a close. No one has ever had the longevity in major championship golf that Jack had. He is the greatest champion who ever lived.

Tiger Woods

The Venue

Keys To The Old Course

By Michael McDonnell

It is the ability to adapt technique and attitude that distinguishes champions at St Andrews on the Old Course, which demands a new and subdued approach to playing golf even among the greatest players.

Some 70 years ago the eminent golf course architect Alister MacKenzie took issue with that rather familiar observation concerning the Old Course that its reputation is based on tradition rather than merit and its place in history masks fundamental playing defects.

In his book *The Spirit of St Andrews*, discovered many years after his death, he wrote, "My experience is exactly the opposite. I am by nature a revolutionary and only too apt to scoff at tradition. Before visiting St Andrews I had what were considered revolutionary ideas concerning golf courses. To my astonishment when I inspected the Old Course I found my ideas in actual practice."

Thus the creator of some 400 golf courses around the world including the masterpieces of Cypress Point and (jointly with Bobby Jones) Augusta National came to the conclusion that this stretch of seaside terrain in the Kingdom of Fife held a enduring relevance to the principles of contemporary golf course design even though it had existed in basic form for centuries without much intervention.

Indeed MacKenzie observed that what he called the "much abused old course" had so far "escaped destruction by vandals in the shape of amateur golf architects ... partially owing to the fact that the members have considered it too sacred to be touched."

Perhaps the conflict of opinion is to be found in the image the Old Course presents of itself as a rather featureless and forbidding piece of landscape which seems to lack the breathtaking beauty of more majestic sweeps of Scottish coastline. Such a view, however, was not held by Andrew "Andra" Kirkaldy, who followed Old Tom Morris in his employment at St Andrews.

The Swilcan Bridge before The Royal and Ancient Golf Club is one of the most familiar scenes in golf, as are the humps and hollows (preceding pages) of the Old Course.

The tee of the 14th hole was extended 37 yards to bring the Beardies bunkers into play.

my knowledge of the course enabled me to play it with patience and restraint until she might exact her toll from my adversary who might treat her with less respect and understanding."

Alister MacKenzie commented approvingly on the manner Jones put this philosophy into effect by deciding, for example, not to try to reach the green with his second shot at the Road Hole 17th for fear of running over on the road behind, but instead playing just short of the green then chipping up for his 4. However, Jones threw caution to the wind in a hard-fought encounter with Cyril Tolley in the fourth round of the 1930 Amateur Championship and went for the green too strongly, but was fortunate enough to hit a spectator and saved from the perils of the road. He beat Tolley in extra time.

The ability to show saint-like self-restraint was never better demonstrated than when two of the most flamboyant characters of the modern game, whose personal style consisted of overwhelming golf courses with their power and daring, emerged as champions at St Andrews. Seve Ballesteros (1984) and John Daly (1995) were rewarded for their self-discipline and respect, but it was Daly's inventiveness as much as his power and patience that earned him the approval of the discerning locals.

On the last hole of the third round, Daly's tee shot landed at the foot of the stone steps leading to The Royal and Ancient Clubhouse and well wide of the green. For Daly, there was only one choice of club, and he reached for his putter to the applause of the crowd and sent the ball on its tortuous journey, thereby demonstrating he had learned how to play the Old Course and how to take his medicine too. He left the ball close enough for a birdie 3.

Ballesteros's triumph in 1984 was Tom Watson's disaster, as the great American golfer, going for his third title in a row and tied with the Spaniard, tried to force the issue in the last round by going for the green with his second on the Road Hole and overshooting the target to lose by two strokes.

One feature of Ballesteros's play that week was the freedom he enjoyed to use the double fairways

Round St Andrews

No 1 • 376 yards Par 4
The tee shot favours the left centre away from the out-of-bounds fence, and the second shot must be played long to avoid the Swilcan Burn which protects the front edge of the green.

No 2 • 453 yards Par 4
A new tee 40 yards back brings Cheape's bunker on the left into play. As the tee shot is blind over hillocks, the need for accuracy is vital, but, once achieved, provides the right angle of attack for the second shot to an undulating green.

No 3 • 397 yards Par 4
A wise tactic is to play the tee shot left to avoid the pot bunkers on the right while still staying short of the Principal's Nose bunker on the left. Although, from this position, the Cartgate bunker guarding the green becomes a threat.

No 4 • 480 yards Par 4
With the tee pushed back 16 yards, the choice is whether to negotiate the narrow valley to provide an easier approach or take the more defensive route over the ridge to the left of the valley, then tackle a cluster of bunkers en route to the green.

No 5 • 568 yards Par 5
The line for the tee shot is on the far-off bunkers, the Spectacles, to the left and well out of range. Downwind, the ridge in front of the green can be carried; but head on, a lay-up is the best policy.

No 6 • 412 yards Par 4
Bunkers flank either side of this fairway to menace the tee shot, so absolute accuracy is required, after which a gully in front of the green presents its own problems and often requires a judicious chip-and-run third shot.

No 7 • 390 yards Par 4
The big tee shot carries the gorse bushes ahead and to the right, but runs the risk of finding the undergrowth, so that the more prudent line is almost certainly straight down the middle to aim for a green that is protected by pot bunkers.

No 8 • 175 yards Par 3
Observe the golden rule of St Andrews and go long with the shot, because all the trouble is at the front of the green, as on so many Old Course greens. Depending on wind strength and direction, it can require anything from a nine iron to a two iron.

No 9 • 352 yards Par 4
The safe line for the shot is wide and to the right of Boase's bunker, leaving a simple pitch—perhaps even a long putt—to a circular green which has no obvious means of protection.

No 10 • 380 yards Par 4
The aim is between the twin bunkers left and Boase's bunker right, and a modest hillock in front of the green presents its own problems, particularly to the aggressive tee shot. Otherwise, the approach must be precisely played, because the green slopes towards the back.

No 11 • 174 yards Par 3
The green drops savagely towards the front, and two greenside bunkers—Hill and Strath—add to the menace. Thus the tee shot must be judged to a precise length to leave an uphill putt and aimed exactly to avoid terrifying attempts across the slopes.

No 12 • 348 yards Par 4
An extra 34 yards means that the hidden bunkers in the middle of the fairway are firmly in play from the tee. For those who do not relish the risk, then a cautious shot to the left of Stroke bunker is required.

No 13 • 465 yards Par 4
A new tee 35 yards back means the carry over the Coffins bunkers is now 285 yards and probably not worth the risk unless downwind. There is broken ground in front of the green, so the approach cannot land short but must find the target.

No 14 • 618 yards Par 5
An additional 37 yards bring the Beardies bunkers on the left into play and means the tee shot must find the safety of the landing area between these hazards and the out-of-bounds wall on the right. The wise move is to play left of Hell bunker with the second shot.

No 15 • 456 yards Par 4
The safe line for the tee shot is on the church spire in the distance and between two humps known as Miss Grainger's Bosoms, although the small Sutherland bunker still menaces from the left, providing another reason to play long with the approach to this double green.

No 16 • 423 yards Par 4
The brave line from the tee is between the Principal's Nose bunker on the left and the out of bounds to the right for an easier and straighter approach. The more sensible line is to the left of the bunker, although even this leaves a threatened approach over two bunkers to the left.

No 17 • 455 yards Par 4
The wise strategy is to come up short of the green with the approach to allow a chip-and-run or a putt to get close to the flag. The favoured line from the tee is across the out of bounds of this right-hand dogleg, because a drive too far left imposes the perils of the Road bunker.

No 18 • 357 yards Par 4
The line for the tee shot is towards the clock on the wall of The Royal and Ancient Clubhouse, but from the left side the approach must clear the hollow known as the Valley of Sin, with the flagstick invariably placed in close proximity.

International Final Qualifying

ASIA　6-7 April

Saujana　*Kuala Lumpur, Malaysia*

Mardan Mamat, Singapore	66	71	137
Danny Chia, Malaysia	67	72	139
Richard Moir, Australia	71	68	139

Mardan Mamat

AMERICA　27 June

Canoe Brook　*Summit, New Jersey*

Tom Pernice, USA	64	70	134
Geoff Ogilvy, Australia	67	67	134
Jason Allred, USA	69	66	135
Joe Durant, USA	66	69	135
Duffy Waldorf, USA	68	67	135
Alex Cejka, Germany	67	68	135
Scott Gutschewski, USA	68	67	135
Tom Byrum, USA	68	68	136
Daniel Chopra, Sweden	68	69	137
Robert Allenby, Australia	72	65	137
Scott Hend, Australia	67	70	137
Bo Van Pelt, USA	66	71	137
(P)Wilhelm Schauman, Sweden	71	67	138
(P)Rich Barcelo, USA	67	71	138

Geoff Ogilvy

AUSTRALASIA 25-26 January

Kingston Heath　*Melbourne, Australia*

Peter Fowler, Australia	70	69	139
David Diaz, Australia	69	72	141
Martin Doyle, Australia	73	71	144
(P)Nick Flanagan, Australia	75	70	145

Peter Fowler

St Andrews

EUROPE 27 June
Sunningdale *Berkshire, England*

Simon Khan, England	66	66	132
Peter Lawrie, Ireland	65	67	132
John Bickerton, England	67	66	133
Robert Coles, England	66	68	134
Simon Dyson, England	67	67	134
Marcus Fraser, Australia	65	69	134
Andrew Oldcorn, Scotland	67	67	134
Peter Baker, England	64	70	134
Ian Woosnam, Wales	66	68	134
Alastair Forsyth, Scotland	67	67	134
Patrik Sjoland, Sweden	67	68	135
Andrew Butterfield, England	65	70	135
Robert Rock, England	68	67	135
(P)Kenneth Ferrie, England	68	68	136

Ian Woosnam

AFRICA 13-14 January
Atlantic Beach *Cape Town, South Africa*

David Frost, South Africa	65	76	141
(P)Andre Bossert, Switzerland	66	76	142
(P)Douglas McGuigan, Scotland	69	73	142

David Frost

Tiger's Ominous Warning

By Robert Sommers

With a run of seven birdies over nine holes in the opening hours of his return to the Old Course, Tiger Woods gave notice to all the other competitors that he was prepared to reclaim the prize of the Claret Jug after five years.

Over the history of The Open Championship, which reaches back to the middle years of the 19th century, only four men had won twice over the Old Course at St Andrews—Bob Martin in 1876 and 1885, J H Taylor in 1895 and 1900, James Braid in 1905 and 1910, and Jack Nicklaus in 1970 and 1978.

Many others have won at least once over these historic links, and some of the best not at all. Harry Vardon had never won there, nor had Tom Watson. Although he had won five Open Championships, a number beaten only by Vardon's six, Watson had contended only in 1984.

Tiger Woods made good use of his driver on the shorter par-4s.

On the eve of The Open 2005, only Nicklaus, among the living, had won twice.

Then on an overcast morning in July of 2005, Tiger Woods sped round this ancient ground in 66 strokes and announced he had returned to full power and intended to win a second St Andrews Open as well.

Even though three hard days lay ahead, from the moment he ran off seven birdies over a run of nine holes, from the fourth to the 12th holes, the other 155 men making up the starting field understood quite well they probably could hope for nothing better than second place.

Disheartening perhaps, but five years earlier Woods had played four rounds over this same difficult and perplexing course in 269 strokes, never once scoring as high as 70. He won the Championship by eight strokes, and he had begun with a round of 67. Now, in 2005, he had beaten that opening score by a stroke.

A later comparison of the statistics produced by Unisys, without regard for starting times, showed that when Woods birdied the 11th hole to go to six under par, he passed Steve Webster, who was the

Off at 6.30 am, Simon Dyson was back with a 70, saying, 'I'd love to be first off at every tournament, to be honest.'

Memories *of* St Andrews

Gordon Jeffrey
Former Captain of the R&A

"In a press conference before the 2000 Open, a reporter warned Tiger Woods he would probably lose some strokes in some of those punishing bunkers. Woods replied, 'Then I just won't be in a bunker.' And he wasn't."

last other than Woods to hold or share the lead for the first round or in this Championship week. (Webster was never shown as such on the scoreboards because he started more than four hours after Woods.)

At the end of the day Woods held a one-stroke lead over the surprising Mark Hensby, the Australian golfer who had tied for fifth in the Masters Tournament in April, and tied for third in the United States Open in June. Ten men played the Old Course in 68 strokes, among them Jose Maria Olazabal, Retief Goosen, Luke Donald, Fred Couples, Trevor Immelman, and Eric Ramsay, 25 years of age, an amateur from Scotland. Michael Campbell, the new US Open champion, a New Zealander, and Vijay Singh, and six others scored 69. All told, 20 players broke 70, and that did not include Colin Montgomerie, who started in 71 but would play a major role.

A look at the scoreboard, where Woods sat perched on top at six under par, and Monty described it as "Ominous."

"If ever a course was built for him, this is it."

Indeed, it seemed to be.

Meantime, both Nicklaus and Watson, playing together, along with Donald, matched each other's 75s and faced the possibility they would

First Round Leaders

HOLE	1	2	3	4	5	6	7	8	9	10	11	12	13	14	15	16	17	18	
PAR	4	4	4	4	5	4	4	3	4	4	3	4	4	5	4	4	4	4	TOTAL
Tiger Woods	4	4	4	③	④	4	③	3	③	③	②	③	⑤	5	4	⑤	4	③	66
Mark Hensby	③	⑤	4	4	5	4	4	3	②	③	3	③	4	5	③	4	4	4	67
Retief Goosen	4	4	③	4	④	4	⑤	3	③	③	3	③	⑥	④	4	4	4	③	68
Luke Donald	4	4	③	4	④	4	4	3	③	4	④	4	③	④	4	4	4	4	68
Peter Lonard	4	③	③	⑥	5	4	4	3	③	③	3	⑤	⑥	③	③	4	4	③	68
Jose Maria Olazabal	4	4	4	4	④	4	③	3	③	4	3	4	4	5	4	4	4	③	68
Scott Verplank	③	⑥	③	4	④	4	4	3	③	4	3	4	⑤	④	4	4	③	③	68
Chris Riley	③	4	4	⑤	④	4	4	3	③	4	3	4	4	④	4	4	③	4	68
*Eric Ramsay	4	⑤	4	⑤	5	③	③	3	③	③	④	4	4	④	③	4	4	③	68
Tino Schuster	4	4	③	4	④	4	③	④	③	4	3	4	4	④	4	4	4	4	68
Trevor Immelman	③	③	4	③	5	4	4	3	③	4	3	4	⑤	④	4	4	4	4	68
Fred Couples	4	4	⑤	4	④	4	4	3	③	4	3	③	4	5	4	4	③	③	68

* Denotes amateur

not survive for the final two rounds. Nicklaus had reached the age of 65 determined to play his best in this, his final appearance in The Open. His first round left little question he would bow out after the second. At 55, Watson would be eligible for the next 10 years.

The early starters caught the Old Course in a largely benign mood. Clouds covered the old town much of the morning and a light wind ruffled the higher grasses of the Old Course. Conditions hardly could have been better for scoring then, but the wind picked up once the tide turned, occasionally gusted to 20 miles an hour, and rain fell late in the afternoon.

Nevertheless, the Old Course did not play at its most severe. The R&A and St Andrews Links Trust had added 164 yards to it from the 2000 Open and stretched it out to 7,279 yards, but the difference had little effect on the power players. With the ground dry and hard, balls rolled along as if on an airport runway and made up for the added length.

Nicklaus, Watson, and Donald began their day at 7.47 am. By then Goosen had been out for half an hour, demonstrating scores could be quite low. He

Playing early, Retief Goosen went two under after five holes.

Mark Hensby

Who Is This New Australian?

It is a fact that some of the men who have led The Open, or been near the lead, after the first round are unable to sustain their challenge to the end of the tournament. There was no reason to suspect that would be the case with Mark Hensby, 34 years of age, from Melbourne, Australia. With ties for third in the recent US Open and fifth at the Masters, Hensby appeared to have the right credentials to be a success at St Andrews even if he was something of an unknown player to many golf followers.

If you knew your golf you would have known that when Hensby first arrived in the United States he stayed with friends in Chicago until they moved back to Australia, at which point he was homeless, so he slept in his car at Cog Hill golf course for six weeks. Since joining the PGA Tour in 2001 Hensby had bounced between the Nationwide and PGA Tours.

You would also have noticed his good play at Augusta and Pinehurst in the year's two previous major championships. But would you have known that

in 2004 Hensby had won the John Deere Classic in Illinois the week before The Open, which had entitled him to compete at Royal Troon—an entitlement he then declined because he didn't have a passport at the time? Not only that. Would you have known that this was his first Open and his first tournament in Britain?

Tradition has it that the more you play the Old Course the better you get at it. Put it another way: Until you have played the Old Course a few times you have no chance of understanding its mysterious rules and rhythms. Hensby is proof that, in this particular matter, ignorance is bliss. He knew he had to play accurate, controlled golf, and if he did, then he would get round in a decent score. That is precisely what he did.

While Tiger Woods was in three bunkers (compared with none at all during his 2000 Open victory) and Steve Webster was in six on his inward nine holes alone, Hensby steered his ball to the correct positions on the fairways from where he was able to attack the flags that he wanted to attack and to put his ball into safe positions on the

large greens when he wanted to do that. It was almost a faultless round.

His game was as neat as a pin: one missed green (the second) for his only bogey of the day, an eagle on the ninth which, like so many others, he reached with a booming drive, and birdies on the first, 10th, 12th, and 15th. He found 12 of the 16 fairways from the tee and hit 15 greens in the correct number of strokes. His shortest putt was a 10-footer on the 10th, his longest a 20-footer on the ninth. The others were 15 feet on the first, 10 feet on the 10th, and two 13-footers on the 12th and 15th. It all added up to a 67 that was compiled without fuss and fanfare and concluded just before 7.30 pm.

"People kept telling me it's a different form of the game, but you still have to hit it in the correct spot like every other form of golf," Hensby said. "Major championships are about having a good short game and I'm usually good around the greens."

—John Hopkins

Peter Lonard took a bogey after this drive into the rough at the 12th. His 68 included two double bogeys, one eagle, and seven birdies.

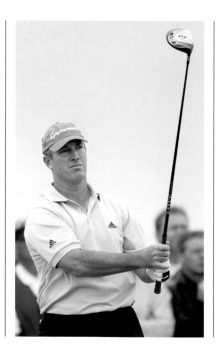

began with a rush, birdieing five of the first 12 holes, but he stumbled on the 13th, a testing par-4 of 465 yards with a blind approach. He drove into one of the Coffins bunkers, which caused so much damage throughout the day, took two more strokes to find the green, and three-putted for a double-bogey 6. He had gone out in 34, two under par, picked up birdies on the 10th, one of the shorter par-4s, the 12th, with a drive and a 60-yard approach to 10 feet, and the 14th, a 618-yard par-5 where he reached the green with his second shot. He completed his round of 68 with a drive and two putts for birdie 3 at the 18th.

With his background—he had won two US Opens —Goosen appeared a legitimate contender. Todd Hamilton, the 2004 champion, did not. Grouped

Mark Hensby's confidence stemmed from his belief in his short game.

Excerpts
FROM THE Press

"The only time Eric Ramsay looked a little out of his depth was when faced with the TV lights and 40 journalists in The Open press tent interview room."
—**Steve Scott,** *The Courier & Advertiser*

"The giants of the game praised (Luke) Donald's fortitude, for they knew how much pressure was on him as the biggest gallery on the course … focused on the past rather than the future."
—**Bob McKenzie,** *Daily Express*

"Zach Johnson suffered the worst case of road rage, posting a 9 on the Road Hole. Sandy Lyle managed to avoid the wicked bunker. But his drive almost landed in the hotel, and his approach shot settled on the 18th tee. 'That was a quick seven,'" he said.
—**Bill Nichols,** *Dallas Morning News*

"There was a moment—not long after 11 o'clock in the morning of the first round—when The Open looked over before half the field had struck a ball, when Woods went to seven under on the 12th."
—**Jeff Powell,** *Daily Mail*

"Colin Montgomerie started the day in the drink—and ended it with the toast of five wacky Monty look-alikes. A group of wig-wearing teenagers from Dunblane declared their support for the fiery Scot with 'We love you Monty' t-shirts and blonde curly perms."
—**Iain Macfarlane,** *Daily Star*

'The ball rolls beautifully,' Scott Verplank reported.

For his 69, Miguel Angel Jimenez birdied the last hole.

Thomas Levet scored a 69 with an eagle 3 on the 14th.

the green because the bunker's revetted face rises straight up considerably higher than one might expect. Some players have trouble seeing over it.

Miss the green to the right and deal with a shot off a tarmacadam road if you're lucky, or from against a stone wall if you aren't.

It is an altogether frightening hole that cost more than one man dearly. Even a putt can be dangerous. Misplayed, it could tumble into the bunker. It has been done.

The 17th played by far as the most difficult hole of all. The field averaged 4.64 strokes, higher than all but the two par-5s. It surrendered just nine birdies and only 72 pars, but it claimed 51 bogeys, two fewer than the 13th, and 16 scores of 6, two more than the 13th. Seven players scored 7s, and one, the American Zach Johnson, scored 9.

Someone charted the 17th and found that the first 18 games, or 54 players, had played through before Scott Verplank scored a birdie 3. As if the dam had broken, Chris Riley birdied in the next group, but then two and a half hours passed before Joe Ogilvie made another.

Colin Montgomerie made a superb 4 from the road, running his ball across the tarmacadam and up the slope onto the green, then holing his putt.

Ian Poulter said of his trousers, 'I thought it was a nice choice.'

Playing with him, David Toms needed two strokes from the road to reach the green, then two-putted for a 6. Montgomerie scored 71, but Toms came in with 74. The following morning Toms told The R&A he believed his ball may have moved after he addressed his second putt. Since he had not penalised himself, he had turned in a score lower than his correct score, and he should disqualify himself. The R&A accepted his decision.

Montgomerie came in with 71, one under par, and said, "A 71 isn't great," he admitted, "but it's not a disaster. A couple of early birdies tomorrow and suddenly you're three under."

"There are messages, then there are messages. This one said: Don't start engraving the Claret Jug just yet, but make sure the engraver practices his T's and W's."

—**Gary D'Amato,**
Milwaukee Journal Sentinel

"Sometimes the shorthand of Tiger Woods's genius makes you want to laugh out loud; the battle seems so uneven, the odds so loaded and it was like this for much of an astonishing round of 66 yesterday."

—**James Lawton,** *The Independent*

"Steve Webster admitted he should have taken a photo of his name at the top of the leaderboard before he came crashing back down to earth."

—**David McDonnell,** *Daily Mirror*

"US Open champ Michael Campbell could have lost the plot after sticking his tee shot into a bush at the 12th hole. But midday's two-minute silence for the London bombing victims made the New Zealander realise there are far more important things in life than a bad shot."

—**Austin Barrett,** *Daily Record*

"There was a minor panic on the fourth tee, when Tiger (Woods) threw down a broken peg and it was out of reach of the youngsters outside the ropes. The marshals stepped in to decide who got the precious relic."

—**Matthew Pinsent,** *The Times*

Round of the **Day**

THE OPEN CHAMPIONSHIP 2005
ST ANDREWS

THIS ROUND _____ **66**

ROUND I
18 HOLE TOTAL
66

Tiger WOODS
Game 11
Thursday 14 July at 8.20 am

ROUND I

Hole	1	2	3	4	5	6	7	8	9	Out
Yards	376	453	397	480	568	412	390	175	352	3603
Par	4	4	4	4	5	4	4	3	4	36
Score	4	4	4	3	4	4	3	3	3	32

Hole	10	11	12	13	14	15	16	17	18	In	Total
Yards	380	174	348	465	618	456	423	455	357	3676	7279
Par	4	3	4	4	5	4	4	4	4	36	72
Score	3	2	3	5	5	4	5	4	3	34	66

After his 66 to start The Open Championship, there was a sense that Tiger Woods should have done better. He was seven under par through 12 holes. "But finishing at six is a great start to the tournament," Woods said. "I'm very pleased with the way I played all day."

Woods hit wedges to the greens on six holes. He got his first birdie after a wedge to 20 feet at the 480-yard, par-4 fourth hole. He then two-putted from 30 feet for another birdie on the par-5 fifth. At the par-4 seventh, Woods hit a three-wood tee shot into a bunker but recovered with a wedge to four feet for his third birdie of the day. He was out in 32 after he drove the green on the 352-yard, par-4 ninth and two-putted from 90 feet.

That was the first of four birdies in succession. Woods pitched to eight feet on the 10th, hit a six iron to 15 feet on the par-3 11th, and pitched again to eight feet on the 12th. Then Woods made bogeys on the 13th and 16th holes after hitting into bunkers, giving him a total of three bunkers hit on the day, whereas he was not in a single bunker when he won here in 2000. His final birdie was on the 18th, where he drove the green and took two putts from 70 feet.

Defending champion Todd Hamilton made birdies on three of the last four holes to finish on 74, two over par.

rolled into one of the Coffins bunkers and left him nothing but a saving shot out, and he bogeyed. A 335-yard drive avoided the Beardies on the 14th, but his second, a shot of 290 yards, pulled up short, leaving him 30 yards from the green.

As he approached his ball, sirens blared throughout the town. Traffic stopped, players and spectators alike stood quietly motionless and observed two minutes of silence in respect of bombing victims of the 7 July terrorist attacks in London.

Woods had been affected more than most. His mother, Kultida Woods, had booked into a London hotel close to one of the bombing sites. She had

Woods made par on the 17th with an iron off the tee.

Nicklaus Steals The Show

By Robert Sommers

It was still Tiger Woods's championship to win, but the second day belonged to Jack Nicklaus and the crowds that cheered on every hole for the final round of an Open career that included three victories, two at St Andrews.

Rare have been the moments when a man on the brink of dominating of one of golf's great events played second fiddle to another about to miss the 36-hole cut. In The Open Championship's second round, Jack Nicklaus did precisely that to Tiger Woods as he marched through those last holes in this, his last appearance in a championship he cherished.

As Nicklaus battled to turn this into more than a ceremonial affair and fought to squeeze one more great score from his game, there behind him, Woods, his logical successor as the world's premier golfer, closed in on a round of 67 and a solid four-stroke lead with 36 holes to play.

Jack Nicklaus played in 141 Open Championship rounds.

At the moment, though, the current Open took on secondary meaning. The great gallery looked to the past, for this had been an emotional day, the last farewell to a dominant and well-liked figure.

Nicklaus had played in 38 Opens, 36 of them consecutively, beginning with his first, in 1962, the year he won the first of his four United States Opens by beating Arnold Palmer in a playoff, and ending in 1996. He returned in 2000, and now again in 2005. Over this long period, Nicklaus had won three Opens including two here at St Andrews in 1970 and 1978, and had placed second in seven others, among them the 1977 Open, certainly the most gripping and dramatic episode of recent times. It was at Turnberry that he and Tom Watson, the two best players of their time, played a calibre of golf others could only dream of. They had played stroke-for-stroke through the first three rounds, but Watson bested Nicklaus by one stroke at the end, 65 to 66.

Now, Nicklaus had reached the end of his career in championship golf. Coming down those last few holes he struggled to survive the 36-hole cut and failed. He thought he had a chance as late as the 17th, but

2

Excerpts
FROM THE Press

As Ian Poulter teed off at the 15th at two over par, the position looked ominous for connoisseurs of the most outlandish wardrobe in golf.… Four birdies on the last four holes changed all that, leaving Poulter to continue his lavishly-gelled drive to make golf cool."

—**Neil Squires,** *Daily Express*

"Sandy Lyle started the day worrying whether he would make the cut, but those thoughts were quickly banished when he fired five birdies in the outward half to be 32 at the turn."

—**Alan Wilson,** *The Courier & Advertiser*

"Both Vijay Singh and fellow big-game hunter Phil Mickelson reckon things could get really interesting if the wind suddenly starts to blow. The Old Course has been remarkably calm so far."

—**Dave Armitage,** *Daily Star*

"Lloyd Saltman says he owes caddie Mark Crane 10 drinks for keeping his Open dream alive. The amateur looked doomed when he had to hit two provisional balls off the 17th. But eagle-eyed Crane found the original ball to avoid a horrendous score."

—**Robert Martin,** *The Sun*

"Ernie Els had a point to prove after his first-round 74. It left the South African in danger of missing a first Open cut since his amateur days at Royal Troon in 1989.… His response was a five-under-par 67."

—**Graham Otway,** *Daily Mail*

Luke Donald (left) and Tom Watson (centre) shared the day with Nicklaus.

when he bogeyed there, he knew his competitive days had ended.

The gallery cared about none of that. On every hole they applauded, happy for this one last sight of him. He marched up that final fairway before two grandstands overflowing with spectators, crowds that lined Links Place, the street running parallel to the fairway, and others watching through open windows of private houses and of the St Andrews Golf Club, and from the balconies of Rusacks Hotel and Forgan House.

In the end Nicklaus went out as a champion should; he holed from 14 feet and birdied the home hole. When the putt fell, the roar sounded throughout the golf course. Those blocked from a view of the 18th green didn't need to see it to know Jack had holed his putt for a level-par 72. But his 36-hole score of 147 missed making the cut by two strokes.

Friday Weather

Mostly cloudy with a variable westerly breeze.

Tiger Woods, teeing off on the sixth hole, played the second round in 67, five birdies and no bogeys.

Second Round Leaders

HOLE	1	2	3	4	5	6	7	8	9	10	11	12	13	14	15	16	17	18	
PAR	4	4	4	4	5	4	4	3	4	4	3	4	4	5	4	4	4	4	TOTAL
Tiger Woods	4	4	③	4	④	4	4	3	③	③	3	4	4	④	4	4	4	4	67-133
Colin Montgomerie	③	4	③	4	③	4	4	④	③	③	3	⑤	⑤	④	③	4	4	③	66-137
Trevor Immelman	4	⑤	③	⑤	5	4	4	3	③	4	3	③	⑤	④	4	4	4	③	70-138
Vijay Singh	③	4	4	4	5	4	4	3	③	4	3	4	4	④	4	4	4	4	69-138
Brad Faxon	4	③	③	4	④	4	4	②	③	4	3	4	4	5	4	4	4	③	66-138
Peter Lonard	4	4	③	4	5	③	⑤	3	③	4	⑤	4	4	5	③	③	⑤	③	70-138
Jose Maria Olazabal	4	4	4	4	5	4	4	3	4	4	④	4	4	④	③	4	⑤	②	70-138
Robert Allenby	4	4	③	4	5	4	③	3	③	4	②	③	4	⑥	4	4	4	4	68-138
Scott Verplank	4	4	③	⑦	③	4	4	②	4	③	3	4	4	④	4	⑤	⑤	③	70-138
Sergio Garcia	4	4	③	⑤	④	4	4	3	⑤	③	3	③	4	5	4	4	4	③	69-139
Fred Couples	4	4	4	4	5	4	4	3	4	4	④	③	4	5	③	⑤	4	③	71-139
Bo Van Pelt	4	4	4	4	④	4	4	②	③	③	3	⑤	4	④	③	4	4	4	67-139
Bart Bryant	4	4	4	4	5	4	4	3	③	4	3	4	4	5	4	4	4	③	70-139
Simon Khan	4	4	4	4	④	4	4	3	③	4	④	③	⑤	④	4	4	4	4	70-139

With 65, David Frost improved 12 strokes.

Richard Green took a bogey at the 17th from the rough.

With tears on his cheeks, he strode off the course into the arms of his family and left the championship to others.

It had been a stirring day indeed, not only with Nicklaus's adieu but with a series of low rounds as well, some from those not among the leaders.

Woods remained in the lead with 133, which was 11 under par, and Colin Montgomerie moved into second place at 137 after a stirring round of 66. Seven others tied at 138, a group that included Brad Faxon, who matched Montgomerie's 66. Vijay Singh had a second 69 and lost ground, along with Robert Allenby, with 68, and Trevor Immelman, Peter Lonard, Jose Maria Olazabal, and Scott Verplank, all with 70s.

Meantime, Mark Hensby, who had trailed Woods by one stroke going into the second round, posted a 77 and dropped from second place into a tie for

Trevor Immelman returned a 70 with a birdie at the last.

Bo Van Pelt posted a 67 to be five under par.

Robert Allenby's 68 put him in the tie for third place.

Memories of St Andrews

Jack Nicklaus
Three-times Open champion

"The final day in 1978 was the best I've ever had in golf. There were three times that I've had where the people were just unbelievable. I'd say four now. There was '78 here, '72 at Muirfield, and '80 at Baltusrol, where the people just absolutely went bonkers over what went on. I was caught up in what was going on with it. And today was equally nice, and it's fantastic."

Jack Nicklaus

The Fondest Farewell To The Greatest Golfer

By David Davies

No golf course, certainly, and few sporting arenas anywhere in the world can have heard anything like it. The citizens of St Andrews, interspersed with golf fans from all around the globe, rose as one on Friday afternoon to say farewell to Jack Nicklaus, the greatest player the game has ever known.

Rarely, if ever, can such a volume of noise have been sustained for so long. The tens of thousands packed into the grandstands behind the 17th green, alongside the first fairway, behind the 18th green, and all along the road to the right of the 18th began their ferocious acknowledgement of the great man's great deeds as he left the 17th green, and 20 minutes later it was undiminished as he disappeared into the recorder's hut to check a Championship card for the last time.

There had been pauses, of course. The

silence was infinite as Nicklaus took rather longer than usual to approach his final drive off the 18th tee. The body language was completely clear—this one had to be good.

When he finally got to the ball he addressed his tee shot with his customary three waggles, with his usual tilt of the head to the right, with his normal deliberate takeaway leading to that famous flying right elbow, and then the hit and the quizzical look as he followed the flight.

It was a good one, almost his best, but unlike the monsters he unleashed in 1978, when he drove the green of this 357-yard hole, this was probably 40 yards short of the putting surface. But it was still a good one. Jack said later he was pleased, and the crowded balconies over the cashmere shop of Johnstons of Elgin, over the Tom Morris golf shop, and of Rusacks Hotel, gave it a fervent thumbs-up. So, too, the members of

The Royal and Ancient Golf Club crammed onto the balcony outside the office of the Secretary Peter Dawson. Among them, cheering as ardently as anyone, the 2004 Captain of the Club, Prince Andrew.

There were to be further pauses in the noise. Nicklaus, his playing partners Tom Watson and Luke Donald, posed on the Swilcan Bridge, and Jack, who in his final interview later that day called himself "a sentimental old fool" on no fewer than three occasions, could not contain his emotions.

Perhaps it was because his eyes were still full or, more prosaically, because he has never been the world's best with a wedge, he decided to putt his second shot through the Valley of Sin, hit it a little too hard, and ran it 14 feet past. Then, although they were nearer, Watson and Donald finished off their rounds, leaving Nicklaus once more poised over a birdie putt on the 18th green at St Andrews.

Let Nicklaus take up the story. "I knew that the hole would move wherever I hit the ball. I always make it on the 18th. I just figure it will go in, so I hit it and it went in."

Bedlam broke out, again. So, too, the tears. Asked what he said to son Steve, caddying for him, Nicklaus replied: "He's as sentimental as I am. He has trouble getting words out, too. We sort of choked a little bit and gagged a little bit and had a couple of

The Royal Bank of Scotland honoured Jack Nicklaus by issuing a special commemorative £5 banknote bearing his image. The note recognized his Open Championship victories at St Andrews in 1970 and 1978. Other than the Queen and the late Queen Mother, Nicklaus was the only living person ever to have appeared on a Scottish note. Two million of the notes were issued. "It's one of the most memorable honours I've had in my career," Nicklaus said.

Nicklaus in 1978, and now on the money.

tears and hugged each other—sort of like that."

The tears were not confined to Nicklaus and family. There were few dry eyes in this house, in the incredible amphitheatre formed around the first and 18th holes of this unique golf course. There was, for instance, another former Open champion making his last appearance in this event. He had completed his round, had missed the cut, and was being interviewed one last time on the gantry overlooking the course.

But it was too much for Tony Jacklin, winner of The Open in 1969 and the US Open in 1970. The two men have history, and a brilliant one at that, going back to the Ryder Cup of 1969 when Nicklaus conceded the two-foot putt that meant a tie between the teams. Perhaps there was one tear for Jack and one for his own passing from the scene, but he definitely contributed to what was, if there can be, a joyfully lachrymose occasion.

Away from the adulation, Nicklaus, facing the press, had regained control of himself. But as he sat there, it was evident that the emotional strains and stresses of the past week had taken a toll. There comes a time in everyone's life when physical signs cannot be ignored: the creaking knees and hips, the wrinkles by the eyes, the receding hairline.

Nicklaus has reached that stage, and he was delighted that when it came to it in that second round he managed to play his best golf of the year. "This year," he said, "in my eight competitive rounds, I've shot 75, 76, 75, 77, 73, 77, 75, 72, and that's not great golf. My biggest fear coming here was that I didn't want to finish shooting a pair of 80-somethings. So 72 is the best round I shot this year. I played well and I'm missing the cut by two shots. When that happens you know it's time to leave.

"Actually, as I was coming down the last few holes, I'm saying, man, I don't want to go through this again. Maybe it's just as well I miss the cut. I said, I think these people have been wonderful. They've given of themselves and gave me a lot more than I deserved. I'm probably better off getting out of here. Obviously I kept trying to do the best I could."

And so, just short of 6 pm on Friday 15 July 2005, it was all over, and now Jack Nicklaus can go fishin', instead of just a' wishin'.

Watson and Nicklaus left as they had after their duel in 1977 at Turnberry.

Excerpts FROM THE Press

"The scene here provided the perfect stage for Jack Nicklaus to leave—the only way the best golfer, the best competitor, and the best sportsman of our time could leave."

—Dave Anderson, *The New York Times*

"It was no surprise when Jack Nicklaus compressed time at the home of golf with one final perfect stroke that represented all the competitive magic he brought to major championships for nearly half a century."

—Dave Shedloski, PGATOUR.com

"In 45 years of playing the game, Jack Nicklaus has received many ovations in golf. The only question is: Will he ever be able to remove from his mind the one he received last night coming down the final fairway of his final Open? In sport's cynical and coarse age, there are still some authentically beautiful scenes, and Nicklaus bowing out on the 18th at St Andrews surely qualifies among the finest."

—Graham Spiers, *The Herald*

"When there was no more golf to play, the tears had dried and cheers had blown away in the breeze, Jack Nicklaus was asked what he would do differently in a golf life like no other. 'I can't think of anything,' Nicklaus answered."

—Ron Green Jnr, *The Charlotte Observer*

Clockwise from bottom left, American newcomer Sean O'Hair returned a 67; Hiroyuki Fujita was the leading Japanese player after 36 holes; Brad Faxon brought star quality to the Local Final Qualifying, then started with 72 and 66, tied for third place.

and the scoring responded. Of the field of 155 players, 30 scored in the 60s.

Off early in the day, Trevor Immelman went round in 70 and caught Woods at six under par. The hitch was that Woods hadn't started yet. Nevertheless, it has been a decent follow-up to Immelman's opening 68, and at the end of the round he joined those others in the third-place tie at 138.

Vijay Singh was among them. Possibly the second best player in the game, Singh struggled with his driver through the first two rounds, and yet his iron play in the second had been immaculate. He hit every green except the 10th, and that only because his approach had run off the back. He had actually driven the ninth and holed in two from 50 feet. No, it wasn't his long game, he had been betrayed by his putting. He simply could not decipher those puzzling greens. As he left the second green perplexed, he asked Furyk if his putt, as Vijay's, had broken first left, then right.

Opening with a 69, at day's end Singh had trailed Woods by just three strokes, and he began the second round with a birdie at the first. Then the drought began. Over the next five holes he gave himself birdie openings from inside 10 feet, 12 feet, 20 feet, six feet, and 12 feet again, yet missed them all.

Asked about it later, Singh said, "It's not that I wasn't stroking it (the ball) well, it was just not going in." He added that the pace of the greens had been slower than in the first round, possibly because of the afternoon rain the previous day.

Singh turned in another 69 for his 138 and said later, "You make some, you miss some. Hopefully over the weekend I can make some."

While Singh had gone along steadily, Brad Faxon had played his first round in level-par 72 and bettered it by six strokes in the second. Faxon had taken an unusual route into The Open. Not high enough in the world rankings for an exemption but nevertheless wishing to play, he flew over to Scotland and entered one of the Local Final Qualifying events, competing against 90 others for three places in The Open. He qualified, and told the story of how about 40 members of Lundin, the qualifying site, had formed a gallery and followed him as he played a practice round.

"That was a great feeling," he said, "because it doesn't happen to me often."

It certainly should have this day, because Faxon played outstanding golf, breezing through the outward nine in 31 strokes with five birdies, and the homeward nine in 35 with a birdie on the last. He hadn't lost a single stroke. His 31 was just one stroke above Steve Webster's 30 in the opening round, but Webster had come back in 41. Faxon had held steady.

Vijay Singh 'left a lot of shots out there.'

Excerpts
FROM THE **Press**

"It also takes a special kind of sportsman to retire from The Open twice, and for those who may have forgotten, the Saturday morning papers in 2000 were also full of pictures of Nicklaus waving his farewells from the Swilcan Bridge."

—**Martin Johnson,** *The Daily Telegraph*

"It usually doesn't take much to irritate Colin Montgomerie, but he ignored the distractions that came his way and put himself in contention at St Andrews."

—**Phil Johnson,** *The Scotsman*

"Vijay Singh, at least, knows what it is like to catch and pass Tiger Woods."

—**Richard Edmondson,**
The Independent

"As an example of course management at its best, Singh's round could not be faulted. He is familiar with the Old Course … and brings his experience to bear in choice of club and angle of attack."

—**Peter Dixon,** *The Times*

"The American (Brad Faxon) insisted that even if he'd shot two 76s, the trip would have been worth it. Because this is where golf was born, you see, and Faxon knows he owes his existence to this very place."

—**David McCarthy,** *Daily Record*

"Colin Montgomerie will go head-to-head with Tiger Woods in a bid to stop the American walking away with The Open title—and land his own elusive first major at the grand old age of 42."

—**Neil McLeman,** *Daily Mirror*

Phil Mickelson had a crowd-pleasing 67, seven shots better than his first round.

Stuart Appleby scored a 68 despite bogeys on the 16th and 17th holes.

Players Below Par	74
Players At Par	19
Players Above Par	62

Two steady rounds of 71 and 69 had Bernhard Langer tied for 15th place, seven strokes back.

only six birdies. And he should know as well that two others played it at least as badly.

From then on Hensby was a model of consistency, playing the remaining 14 holes in one under par, courtesy of a birdie on the home hole. From 67 to 77, Hensby nevertheless made the cut.

Montgomerie did better than that, certainly. With a 66 of his own, he vaulted into second place, at 137, four strokes behind Woods and a stroke ahead of the seven others who tied for third.

Monty stepped on the first tee determined to change tactics for the opening hole and wasted no time in attacking the course. In the first round he had pulled his first tee shot into the Swilcan Burn and lost a stroke right away, but now he drove with an iron, pitched on to eight feet, and holed for a birdie 3. After a safe par 4 at the second, he picked up another stroke on the third, holing from four feet. Then he made his biggest move on the fifth, the easier of the two par-5s. A solid drive, then a three iron that cleared the chasm before the green and bounded on within 12 feet of the hole. He holed it for an eagle 3.

Four under for the day then, he gave one stroke back by missing

Memories of St Andrews

Peter Thomson
Five-times Open champion

"I played the British match play in September of 1954, a monumental match against John Panton, the pride of Scotland. Two down with two holes to play, I won on the fourth extra hole with a putt from 30 yards as a haar rolled in and darkness fell."

In the *Words* of the **Competitors…**

"(Ernie Els) is an unbelievable bloke. I was so relaxed. His body language and his attitude just rub off on you. I must have carried that on through these first two days."

—Amateur Matthew Richardson

"I'm very familiar with the golf course. If there was an Open Championship I was going to win, then it would probably be round this golf course…. But still you've got to go out and make the shots."

—Vijay Singh

"Yes, I made a nice putt (on the 18th) from the front edge for eagle, and I'm hoping I'm in for the weekend. I left a lot of shots out there, and I was due for something good to happen."

—Tom Lehman

"Coming over here to qualify got me in the spirit, and I hope it carries through the next few days."

—Brad Faxon

"I think there are some guys out there who can stay within four or five of the lead, and at the weekend anything can happen."

—David Frost

After this drive, Colin Montgomerie had two putts from 25 yards for a 66 with a birdie on the home hole.

the eighth green, then drove the green of the ninth and got down in two from 60 feet. Four under for the nine holes now.

Out in 32, he dipped to five under par by birdieing the 10th as well, but he lost strokes on both the 12th and 13th. Monty closed with three birdies on the last five holes and came back in 34.

Montgomerie had played solid golf throughout the day. He had hit 12 of the 16 fairways, 15 of the 18 greens, and with eight one-putt greens, he had seldom putted better. Now he would see if he could keep up the pace.

Because David Toms had disqualified himself early that morning, Montgomerie and Paul Lawrie had played alone, and when Monty saw a news item on television explaining Toms's withdrawal, he became concerned and explained, "I signed his card last night, and I thought, 'What have I done now?'" a reference to his disputed replacement of a ball in Jakarta four months earlier.

Italy's Edoardo Molinari was the leader among the four amateurs who survived.

It's a Fact

Four amateurs survived the 36-hole cut, which came at 145, one over par. They were Edoardo Molinari (Italy), Eric Ramsay (Scotland), Matthew Richardson (England), and Lloyd Saltman (Scotland). The last time four amateurs made the cut was at St Andrews in 1995, when Steve Webster (England) won the Silver Medal. The others were Gordon Sherry (Scotland), Tiger Woods (USA), and Gary Clark (England).

Tiger Enjoys Being In Jack's Shadow

"I wish he would keep retiring. It's been very good so far."

Tiger Woods has got used to being overshadowed by Jack Nicklaus when Nicklaus is making a farewell from the game he has adorned so well for so long. Each time, Woods has won. It happened at three championships of 2000, the US Open, The Open Championship (which Nicklaus said then was probably his last), and the USPGA Championship, and again at the 2005 Masters Tournament. And it happened on the second day at St Andrews this year.

"It's been good every time he's retired," Woods had said in his press conference at the start of the week. "I wish he would keep retiring. It's been very good so far."

As Nicklaus was coming up the 18th and thousands of people gathered down the side of the first, on the balconies of The Royal and Ancient clubhouse, behind the 18th green, and in vantage positions down the right-hand side of the 18th to acclaim him for what he had done for golf and The Open, Woods was three holes and 33 minutes behind. The wind, such as it was, was blowing Woods home, so much of the tumult that greeted Nicklaus up ahead was out of Woods's earshot.

The younger American heard enough of what his older countryman was doing nonetheless. "To be compared to the greatest champion that has ever lived in our game, it's nice to be in that company and mentioned in that kind of breath," Woods said. "He's been the benchmark for every player that has ever played the game.

"I would have loved to have gone head-to-head against him in his prime. I think we would have had a lot of fun."

Having left his rivals struggling to keep up with him in the first round, when he went round in 66, the world No 1 pressed his foot to the accelerator in the second and went round in 67. The result was that he widened his one-stroke lead overnight to four at the

For Woods, the cameramen are never far away, nor are the photographers.

halfway stage of the competition. It was a composed and merciless demonstration, an echo of his first two rounds five years earlier when he had started with a 67 and followed it up with a 66 to lead by three strokes.

Woods seemed full of resolve, determined to maintain the statistic that showed he had led after 36 holes of five major championships and gone on to win them all—the 1997 Masters, the 2000 US Open, Open Championship and USPGA Championship, and the 2002 Masters.

The round seemed to stand for everything Woods wants his new swing to stand for. It was rhythmical and controlled. There was power aplenty, most notably when he drove the 10th, a shot measured at 380 yards. He had also driven close to the ninth, and as if to demonstrate that he understands that in Scotland the game is meant to be played on the ground as much as possible and in the air as little as possible, his first putt was from 50 yards. There was an extra degree of accuracy that had not been present the day before when shots ran into

three bunkers. This time Woods's feet did not touch sand.

As the Championship leader, as he had been in 2000, Woods was asked whether there were any similarities between then and now. You expected him to answer in the affirmative because there did seem to be a lot of things in common—that he led was one and that his 36-hole total was the same was another. But to Woods, none of this was an echo of his triumph in 2000.

"I couldn't care less [about 2000]," Woods said, reminding us once again how clearly he thinks about the game and how focused he was on the job in hand. "Thinking of 2000 is not going to help me hit a golf shot out there, hit a draw or a high fade. I have to be in the present here and now. I am trying to put the ball in the place where I need to place it and that's it. It doesn't get any more complicated than that."

—John Hopkins

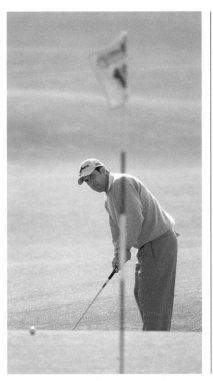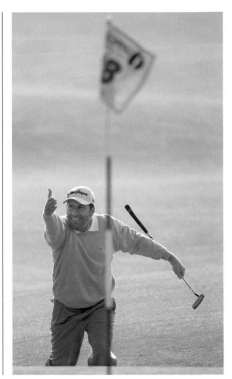

When Jose Maria Olazabal holed out on the 18th, he had a celebration worthy of an eagle 2 for 70, to the delight of all.

Montgomerie and Lawrie had started four groups behind Woods, and when they finished it seemed likely Montgomerie would be paired with him in the third round. Asked if it should be a fun round, Monty said no.

"Everyone says it's fun when Tiger shoots 80, so I'm not going to say it's fun. This isn't fun. This is a major championship. It's a job of work, and it's very much a business. All I can say is I look forward to the whole atmosphere of the day."

Woods certainly did not shoot 80 this day. Instead he sped round the Old Course in 67 strokes and a halfway score of 133, which matched his 36-hole total of five years earlier. It was then he went on to win The Open by eight strokes. Once again, here he wasted no time putting pressure on the rest of the field.

After two routine pars at the start, he pitched to six feet and holed his putt for a birdie on the third, and reached the green of the fifth, which measured 568 yards, with a six-iron second to 25 feet. Two putts and he had his second birdie.

Round Two Hole Summary

HOLE	PAR	YARDS	EAGLES	BIRDIES	PARS	BOGEYS	D.BOGEYS	HIGHER	RANK	AVERAGE
1	4	376	0	29	110	14	2	0	11	3.93
2	4	453	0	22	93	36	3	1	6	4.15
3	4	397	0	32	113	10	0	0	13	3.86
4	4	480	0	6	97	45	4	3	2	4.36
5	5	568	8	73	58	15	1	0	18	4.54
6	4	412	0	21	113	20	1	0	9	4.01
7	4	390	0	25	118	9	2	1	10	3.94
8	3	175	0	16	115	23	1	0	8	3.06
9	4	352	4	73	61	15	2	0	16	3.60
OUT	**36**	**3603**	**12**	**297**	**878**	**187**	**16**	**5**		**35.44**
10	4	380	0	32	117	4	2	0	14	3.85
11	3	174	0	16	98	36	3	2	5	3.21
12	4	348	1	40	96	16	0	2	12	3.88
13	4	465	0	7	96	47	5	0	3	4.32
14	5	618	0	58	73	18	5	1	15	4.83
15	4	456	0	15	106	34	0	0	7	4.12
16	4	423	0	9	111	29	5	1	4	4.21
17	4	455	0	4	70	67	8	6	1	4.63
18	4	357	3	63	83	5	1	0	16	3.60
IN	**36**	**3676**	**4**	**244**	**850**	**256**	**29**	**12**		**36.65**
TOTAL	**72**	**7279**	**16**	**541**	**1728**	**443**	**45**	**17**		**72.08**

Three more pars followed at the sixth through the eighth holes, and now he had arrived at the ninth tee. Woods had driven the green a day earlier and got down in two from 90 feet. He did not so well here. This time he putted from an estimated 50 yards, yet so good is his putting he still got down in two for his third birdie of the first nine.

With the wind in his face playing the 10th, he had driven with a two iron on Thursday, then played a pitching wedge. As he stepped onto the tee Friday, he fully intended to lay up once again, but suddenly the direction of the wind changed and came in slightly behind him. Instead of an iron, Woods pulled out his driver, a club with a shaft 45 inches long topped with one of those huge heads, and whaled it. The ball is estimated to have settled 380 yards from its starting point and about 70 feet from the hole.

"If it had been into the wind," Woods said later, "I couldn't have done it."

Nevertheless, he did do it, and once again got down in two from an unreasonable distance for his fourth birdie of the day. He made his last on the 618-yard 14th with a drive, a three iron, and two putts from 60 feet.

In this round he showed once again that he has more in his arsenal than raw power. As most of the great ones, Woods has a delicate touch around the greens and he is deadly with a putter from 10 feet or so. Those 60- or 70-foot putts don't bother him because he knows he can manoeuver his ball close enough to, more likely than not, hole it.

When he is on his game, as he most certainly had been to this point, he would by dreadfully difficult to beat. Or catch.

Woods missed an eagle attempt at the fifth, but got the birdie.

It's Now A Tiger Hunt

By Robert Sommers

Playing alongside Scots favourite Colin Montgomerie, Tiger Woods failed to break 70 at St Andrews for the first time as a professional, and his lead was cut from four strokes to two, as Jose Maria Olazabal and Retief Goosen also gave chase.

After the first two rounds, when Tiger Woods scored 66 and 67, he seemed unlikely to play a round over the Old Course in more than 69 strokes. This was his second Open Championship as a professional at St Andrews. In his first, five years earlier, he had scored 67, 66, 67, and 69. He kept up the pace in his first 36 holes of the 2005 Championship, running off successive rounds of 66 and 67.

But then all good things end. Woods lost some of his surgical precision overnight and returned a third-round score of 71, still a stroke under par, and still good enough to hold onto his lead, but his

---

With 70, Colin Montgomerie pulled within three strokes.

breathing room had been reduced to two strokes over Jose Maria Olazabal and three over Colin Montgomerie and a revived Retief Goosen.

Woods led with a 54-hole score of 204. Olazabal, with 68, followed at 206. Montgomerie, with 70, and Goosen, matching Woods's opening 66, lay three strokes behind at 207. After them, Sergio Garcia and Brad Faxon were at 208, and Michael Campbell and Vijay Singh trailed with 209. Eleven others tied for ninth place at 210.

Woods and Montgomerie began in the final game just after 3 o'clock, and Monty quickly picked up a stroke when Woods bogeyed the second. He missed the fairway, then three-putted from 50 feet. He made pars on the third and fourth, where he missed another green yet ran the ball close with his putter. Then Woods stepped onto the fifth tee. Holes such as this—a 568-yard par-5—have become easy pickings for the modern professional golfer, and Woods eats them up. A drive of great length followed by a four iron to the green, then a putt from 30 feet that scarcely missed for an eagle. A birdie would have to do.

Montgomerie matched it with a three-iron sec-

Saturday Weather

Sunny periods with a variable westerly breeze.

A drive here at the sixth ran into the gorse, and Tiger Woods had to take a drop with a penalty stroke; he scored a bogey 5.

Again at the ninth, Woods was in the gorse, but saved a par 4.

ond and two putts. Now, though, Woods ran into trouble.

Over the past few years, when he had failed to win anything of great moment, Woods had struggled with his driver. Occasionally he seemed to have swung so hard he threw himself off balance and, consequently, the ball flew off line, most often to the right. So far during the current year he had kept control of his driving and had played superb golf both in winning the Masters and threatening to win the US Open. He didn't in the end, but because of lax putting, not poor driving.

Here, though, on the sixth tee, his drive drifted to the right and ran into a gorse bush. Earlier in the day, Robert Allenby's ball had flown so deeply into the gorse it couldn't be found. Woods's ball was easily found, but it couldn't be played. He took a drop, pitched on, and, with two putts and a penalty stroke, bogeyed once again.

Montgomerie, meantime, had played the sixth

Third Round Leaders

HOLE	1	2	3	4	5	6	7	8	9	10	11	12	13	14	15	16	17	18	TOTAL
PAR	4	4	4	4	5	4	4	3	4	4	3	4	4	5	4	4	4	4	TOTAL
Tiger Woods	4	[5]	4	4	(4)	[5]	(3)	3	4	4	3	(3)	4	5	4	[5]	4	(3)	71-204
Jose Maria Olazabal	4	4	4	4	(4)	4	4	3	(3)	4	3	(2)	[5]	5	4	4	4	(3)	68-206
Retief Goosen	(3)	4	4	4	[6]	4	(3)	(2)	(3)	4	3	4	4	(4)	(3)	(3)	[5]	(3)	66-207
Colin Montgomerie	4	4	4	4	(4)	4	4	3	(3)	(3)	[4]	4	4	5	4	4	[5]	(3)	70-207
Sergio Garcia	[5]	(3)	4	4	(4)	4	4	3	(2)	4	[4]	4	4	(4)	4	[5]	4	(3)	69-208
Brad Faxon	4	4	4	[6]	(4)	(3)	4	[4]	(3)	4	3	4	4	(4)	[5]	(3)	4	(3)	70-208
Michael Campbell	4	(3)	[5]	4	5	[5]	(3)	(2)	(3)	4	[4]	(3)	4	(4)	4	4	4	(3)	68-209
Vijay Singh	[5]	4	[5]	4	(4)	(3)	(3)	[4]	4	4	3	(3)	[5]	(4)	4	4	[5]	(3)	71-209
Soren Hansen	4	4	(3)	4	(4)	4	4	(2)	(3)	(3)	3	(3)	4	[7]	4	4	4	(2)	66-210
Maarten Lafeber	4	4	(3)	4	(4)	4	(3)	(2)	(3)	4	3	4	4	(4)	4	[5]	4	4	67-210
Darren Clarke	(3)	[5]	4	4	(4)	(3)	(3)	(2)	4	[5]	[4]	(3)	(3)	5	4	(3)	4	4	67-210
Kenny Perry	4	4	(3)	(3)	(4)	4	4	3	4	(3)	3	4	4	[6]	(3)	4	4	4	68-210
Sandy Lyle	4	4	4	4	5	4	4	3	(3)	4	3	(3)	[5]	(4)	[5]	(3)	4	(3)	69-210
Sean O'Hair	4	4	4	4	5	4	4	3	(3)	[5]	3	(3)	4	(4)	4	4	4	4	70-210
Bernhard Langer	[5]	[5]	4	(3)	5	(3)	4	3	4	4	3	4	(4)	(3)	4	4	4	4	70-210
Tim Clark	(3)	(3)	(3)	4	(4)	4	4	3	[5]	4	3	(3)	[5]	5	4	[5]	4	4	70-210
John Daly	(3)	(3)	(3)	4	5	4	4	3	4	[5]	3	(3)	[5]	[6]	4	4	4	(3)	70-210
Bart Bryant	4	4	4	(3)	5	4	[5]	3	(3)	[5]	3	(3)	4	5	[5]	4	4	(3)	71-210
Scott Verplank	(3)	4	4	[5]	(4)	4	4	3	[5]	4	3	(3)	[5]	5	[5]	4	4	(3)	72-210

flawlessly, and with his par 4, had gained two strokes on the leader with two-thirds of the holes still ahead of them. He had begun the day four strokes behind, and now he had moved within two.

Woods, of course, would have none of it. A three wood and sand wedge to 18 feet and he birdied the seventh. With the ninth coming up, another birdie appeared inevitable. Instead, Montgomerie drove the green and holed in two from what seemed to be the edge of Fife, while Woods lost another battle with the gorse.

Once again Woods's ball sat just far enough into those spiky branches to force him to choose discretion over chance, take another drop and another penalty stroke, and get on with it. He made his par nonetheless, but Montgomerie had picked up two strokes by going out in 34 while Woods had scored 36, level par, a novelty for him.

On to the 10th. Woods made his par 4, but Montgomerie played a six iron to five feet, holed the putt, and stepped onto the 11th tee within one stroke of the leader. He would climb no closer. He overshot the green with a six iron and bogeyed; Woods parred, and followed up with a drive to the front of the 12th green and birdied again. His lead once more safe, Woods lost another stroke at the

Excerpts
FROM THE Press

"Champions here have controlled their ball flight and mastered the wind. Winning any tournament is about putting well, but here it involves much more. Golfers must think. The Old Course brings old values back into the game—values that a sea breeze worthy of a links enhance."

—**Lorne Rubenstein,** *The Globe and Mail, Toronto*

"Tiger Woods found himself caught in a desperate struggle to maintain control as the wind swept across St Andrews Bay last night."

—**Peter Higgs,** *The Mail on Sunday*

"Six years since a European, let alone British, winner of The Open—or any other major—is a long time, even if the small consolation remains that it has been much worse than this."

—**Bill Elliott,** *The Observer*

"After three trips to the Auld Grey Toon, this Yank has finally come to the conclusion that St Andrews is more reliable than truly resplendent."

—**Barker Davis,** *Washington Times*

"Even some of the players admit that the only person who can beat Tiger Woods around St Andrews is Woods himself."

—**Mark Reason,** *The Sunday Telegraph*

Montgomerie was level par on the second nine, including a par 4 here at the 13th.

Jose Maria Olazabal's 68 included an eagle 2 on the 12th.

Maarten Lafeber went out in 31, finished at 67, tied for ninth.

16th, but he ripped into a three wood on the home hole, two-putted from 50 yards away, and birdied once again.

Montgomerie, meanwhile, had dropped another stroke with his excursion into the Road bunker, but he birdied the 18th as well.

Looking back, Woods said it had been a difficult day.

"The wind started to pick up in the middle of the round. I hit one loose shot on 10, otherwise I hit it decently. But the greens got so hard, and the fairways had gotten harder. Shots on the fairway were sometimes running 80 yards. It's really hard to judge just how much it's going to roll. It became very difficult."

Then, speaking of his very long putt on the 18th, he said, "Monty and I talked about it later, that when I hit the putt I could actually feel the putter shaft flex. That doesn't happen very often."

Quite true, but seeing Woods at the head of the class and showing supreme confidence in himself, that was normal.

Among others who were expected to contend, Singh had opened with a pair of 69s, but he followed with a loose kind of 71 in the third round. He did indeed hit more fairways in the third than during either of his first two rounds, and while he couldn't be expected to reach more greens than his 17 in the second round, he did reach 13, which wasn't bad. But then he bogeyed as many holes (three) as he birdied on the first nine, and had one more birdie (three) than bogeys on the second. He parred only seven holes in an erratic round of 71.

From the first he had complained of his putting,

Sergio Garcia drove the green for an eagle 2 at the ninth, and scored a 69 despite three bogeys.

Low Scores	
Low First Nine	
Maarten Lafeber	31
Low Second Nine	
Mark Hensby	32
Low Round	
Retief Goosen	66
Soren Hansen	66

up 25 that day), and then I three-putted the 16th. Other than that I was happy. I have a chance tomorrow," he said hopefully. Then added, "The course was tougher today and people were struggling. It was nice to see it that way. It made people play their best."

Perhaps that is what inspired Hansen. He came into the third round while not dragging anchor, not lighting any fires either. In his best performance on the European Tour, he had placed third in the French Open, but mostly he played supporting roles.

At 6ft and over 12 stone, Hansen has enough power to handle the difficult courses, borne out by making his best showing in The Open at Muirfield in 2002. While he tied for eighth place there, his 280 matched a group including Garcia, Goosen, and Thomas Bjorn, all four just two strokes behind Els, Thomas Levet, Stuart Appleby, and Steve Elkington, who tied for first place. Els won the playoff.

Here at St Andrews, Hansen, off the tee at 9.15 am, played the first nine in 32 and started back as if he might match the course record of 62. He played one stretch of five holes, from the eighth through the 12th, in 14 strokes, with four 3s and a 2. Six under par then with six holes to play, he made his 4 on the 13th, but his charge ran into a wall. His drive on the 14th landed on the wrong golf course. It

Soren Hansen's wild run to 66 included 14 strokes over five holes plus an eagle 2.

Geoff Ogilvy advanced with 67.

Mark Hensby rebounded to 69.

"There was always a good chance that a few of Tiger Woods's rivals would make a serious forward move, especially in the benign conditions that prevailed on the Old Course, and they did."

—**Nick Pitt,** *The Sunday Times*

"John Daly was just one of a succession of hopefuls who flared bravely but briefly on the leaderboard on a hot and breezy afternoon, but the prospect of the 1995 Open winner being among the pursuing pack on the closing holes this afternoon started the ripples of renewed excitement."

—**Peter Corrigan,**
The Independent on Sunday

"Colin Montgomerie strode up the last to an ovation normally accorded to champions and he rewarded the home crowd with a birdie which gave him a 70 and a three-shot deficit."

—**Alan Campbell,** *Sunday Herald*

"Lloyd Saltman's four-under-par 68 left the Gorebridge youngster in dream world—as well as in contention for the Silver Medal awarded to the low amateur in The Open."

—**Doug Proctor,** *The Sunday Post*

"Jose Maria Olazabal has been working out to improve his strength and his distance, and it seems to have brightened his outlook as well."

—**Marino Parascenzo,**
Insidetheropes.com

Sandy Lyle shared ninth after his 67, 69.

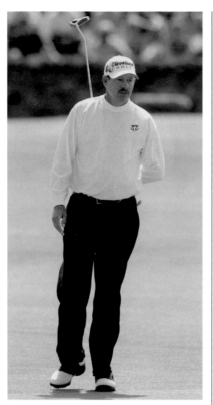

Bart Bryant had stayed close.

Fred Couples had 73 and dropped back.

'It's always special to be here,' John Daly said, and he was not referring to the gorse.

sailed over the stone wall running along the right and settled on the Eden course—out of bounds.

Hansen walked off the green with a 7, a loss of two strokes. All wasn't lost, though. He scored an eagle 2 on the 18th, his second 2 of the round, and posted 66.

About half an hour later, Lafeber began his climb, and once again confounded the fans, who began to wonder what in the world was going on. Before a good many spectators arrived, Lafeber had run up five birdies and made the turn for home in 31 strokes. Five holes later he birdied the 14th as well, looked up, and saw Woods just one stroke ahead of him. Woods, of course, had not yet begun to play.

Lafeber lost a stroke on the 16th, played the second nine in 36, and with 67 slipped into a ninth-place tie.

Goosen teed off just after noon, nearly three hours ahead of Woods. When Goosen birdied the 16th,

Michael Campbell

All About Love And Confidence

Michael Campbell says he loves St Andrews and all about it. "I just really enjoy being here," he says, "being a part of the whole tournament, being part of the atmosphere it creates. Every single tee shot I see out there I like. I feel it's just a wonderful place to play golf."

And yet there is an argument that it was this place that this New Zealander loves that destroyed both his game and his confidence 10 years ago. Destroyed them to the extent that he was known by some on the European Tour as the player with the best swing and the most talent who had not yet achieved.

It was in 1995 that Campbell played a miraculous bunker shot out of the Road Bunker which, in due course, led to him leading The Open after 54 holes. But it was only his second Open Championship and the occasion proved too much for him. After that 65 in the third round, he took 76 to drop back into a tie for third with Steven Bottomley (remember him?) and Mark Brooks.

His obvious promise and high achievement for three rounds at St Andrews ignited even higher hopes, but it was to be 10 very long years before they were fulfilled, at Pinehurst in June when he won the US Open. In the interim, although he won six times on the European Tour, the feeling of underachievement persisted. Had his self-belief and his motivation been permanently dented at St Andrews 1995?

Well, Pinehurst 2005 answered that one adequately and it was confirmed, to some degree, at St Andrews. It was not, of course, that he won, but joint fifth, albeit with Bernhard Langer, Vijay Singh, Geoff Ogilvy, Sergio Garcia, and Retief Goosen, placed him back in the kind of company many felt he should have been keeping in those 10 relatively barren years.

At Pinehurst, shortly after he had beaten back the challenge of Tiger Woods over the closing holes, he found himself in the washroom next to the great man. Exhausted after winning his first major, Campbell said to Woods, who had then won nine, "How do you do this so often?"

It was, of course, an unanswerable question, and Woods merely laughed and said, "Luck, I guess."

Well, Campbell had found out that week at Pinehurst that it was anything but luck, and he had the opportunity at St Andrews to observe, again, how Woods did it.

But his own efforts, certainly after three rounds, had imbued Campbell with the kind of confidence he had maybe lost all those years previous. Listen to him: "I have played well this week. It is not easy a month after winning a major championship to come back and play so well again and prove that you're not just a flash in the pan.

"I'm here for a very long time and I want to win more major championships."

And maybe, after the events of June and July 2005, he will.

—David Davies

he had moved to nine under par, within a stroke of Woods, who by then had bogeyed the second and fallen to 10 under. It didn't last, of course, but Goosen had at least regained his confidence. After his bogey on the fifth, he had said to his caddie, "We're a little bit out of this now."

He had birdied the first, and so he stood level par for the round, but just three under par overall. Quickly, though, Goosen ran off three birdies from the seventh through the ninth. He played a three wood off the seventh tee to stay short of Shell bunker, pitched to 12 feet with his sand wedge, and holed the putt. One under for the day, four under overall.

An eight iron to the eighth and a 20-footer fell, then a drive that missed the ninth green to the right, a chip to seven feet, and another birdie. Out in 33,

Michael Campbell's 68 provided a share of seventh place.

"Tim Clark set the tone of the day with a blistering opening burst. The talented South African birdied the first three holes, producing the kind of display that helped act as a stimulant to all of those busy chasing the Tiger."

—**Brian McNally,** *Sunday Mirror*

"Retief Goosen did what Goosen does; he holed a few putts, got his confidence back and then went for the jugular of the leaders."

—**Tom English,** *Scotland on Sunday*

"While Monty attracted the biggest gallery, those who opted to look elsewhere were wonderfully entertained by Jose Maria Olazabal and Sergio Garcia."

—**Jock MacVicar,** *Sunday Express*

"Ten years ago Jose Maria Olazabal sat slumped in his armchair, remote control in hand as he watched the Golf Channel, wondering if he would ever hit a ball in anger again. A decade later the affable Spaniard is fit, willing and able to finally put that misery behind him as he stands on the verge of glory at the home of golf."

—**Brian McSweeney,** *Sunday Mail*

"Sandy Lyle rolled back the years in front of a raucous Scottish crowd yesterday as a brilliant 69 left him within sight of the leaders."

—**Jim Keat,** *News of the World*

Retief Goosen produced a round of 66 with eight birdies and two bogeys.

he started back with four pars, then began his run for home.

After a big drive on the 14th, his five-iron second settled left of the green, but another deft chip to 15 feet set up still another birdie. Seven under now and moving up. Now a three wood and a sand wedge to three feet on the 15th and another birdie, followed by an unorthodox tactic on the 16th.

A cluster of three bunkers called the Principal's Nose sits squarely in the center of the 16th fairway about 275 yards from the tee. Beyond it lies the widest part of the fairway. Goosen drove into safe ground with his five iron and then played a seven iron to 20 feet and once

Round of the **Day**

THE OPEN CHAMPIONSHIP 2005
ST ANDREWS

Retief GOOSEN
Game 24
Saturday 16 July at 12.15 pm

36 HOLE TOTAL **141**
THIS ROUND **66**
54 HOLE TOTAL **207**

ROUND 3
54 HOLE TOTAL **207**

ROUND 1

Hole	1	2	3	4	5	6	7	8	9	Out
Yards	376	453	397	480	568	412	390	175	352	3603
Par	4	4	4	4	5	4	4	3	4	36
Score	3	4	4	4	6	4	3	2	3	33

Hole	10	11	12	13	14	15	16	17	18	In	Total
Yards	380	174	348	465	618	456	423	455	357	3676	7279
Par	4	3	4	5	4	4	4	4	4	36	72
Score	4	3	4	4	4	3	3	5	3	33	66

Off just after noon, almost three hours ahead of the leader, Retief Goosen needed a spectacular score to become a contender. He matched the second-lowest score of the week with 66, six under par, to enter the final round tied for third place, three strokes behind.

Goosen started well, with a putt for birdie from 15 feet on the first hole, but on the par-5 fifth, he drove into the rough and then hit through the green to take a bogey. "I said to (caddie) Colin (Byrne), 'I think we're out of this now, and we probably need to birdie four of the next five holes.' And I birdied three in a row, and suddenly things started looking better."

The birdies were on a wedge to 12 feet on the seventh, an eight iron to 20 feet on the eighth, and a chip to seven feet on the ninth for Goosen to be out in 33.

After four consecutive pars, Goosen came back in 33 with four birdies and one bogey. He chipped to 15 feet on the 14th, hit a wedge to three feet on the 15th, holed a 20-foot putt on the 16th, three-putted the 17th for the bogey, and on the 18th, hit a three wood and two-putted from 50 feet.

again holed his putt. Now he had climbed to nine under par and had Woods in sight.

That is how he finished. He lost a stroke by three-putting the 17th, but birdied the 18th and came back in 33. He had redeemed his showing of the previous day when he played such pedestrian golf, but he still needed another round such as this to challenge the leaders.

Olazabal moved up the ranks with his second 68. He scored 70 in the second round, giving him 206 for the 54 holes, two strokes behind Woods, and one ahead of Montgomerie and Goosen.

This was Olazabal's fifth Open at St Andrews. He had played there first in 1984 as the Amateur champion, a prize he won at Formby by beating Montgomerie by 5 and 4. He had never won The Open; in his best showing he had placed third in 1992. He had, however, won two Masters Tournaments, his last in 1999. He did not play at Royal Troon in 2004, and he wouldn't have played in 2005 had not Seve Ballesteros withdrawn at the last moment. As the highest listed player in the world ranking, entered but not in The Open, Olazabal filled the vacancy.

Memories of St Andrews

Peter Dawson
Chief Executive, The R&A

"Every morning when I park my car outside the Club and look out on to the first and 18th I still get a buzz. For golfers this is holy ground."

He Didn't Expect To Be Here

"I was very sad," Jose Maria Olazabal said. "I hate to miss The Open."

Jose Maria Olazabal made his debut in The Open at St Andrews in 1984, just a month after defeating Colin Montgomerie in the final of the Amateur Championship at Formby. Some 21 years later, there was an element of symmetry about how the Spaniard and the Scot continued to supply the closest challenge to Tiger Woods as the third round unfolded.

As the Amateur champion all those years ago, Olazabal had played his way into The Open won by Seve Ballesteros thanks to an exemption. In 2005 when the tournament returned, it was the withdrawal of his friend and mentor which opened an unexpected door for the younger Spaniard to compete as the first reserve off the world rankings.

"I certainly didn't expect to be in St Andrews," Olazabal admitted after missing out on one of the places available in International Final Qualifying at Sunningdale. "I was very sad at not making it. I hate to miss The Open, especially when it is at St Andrews. Just because it is what it is.

"I made my first visit to St Andrews in 1984. I remember looking forward to it so much. I knew it was the Mecca of golf. Everyone always told me I had to play the course at some time in my life. After my first round, I have to be honest and say I didn't think much of the place. There were some funny holes. I couldn't work out that I had to hit way over there to finish over here. I never seemed to be on the fairway I thought I should be

on. But the more I played here, the more I appreciated it."

In Saturday's third round, Olazabal, at the age of 39, was expert enough to avoid the mistakes which can scupper a decent score at St Andrews and navigate his way round using the Old Course radar which comes from experience. Apart from a dropped shot at the 13th, where he was bunkered, the two-time Masters champion played beautifully.

After holing a 30-foot putt at the fifth and teasing a lovely little pitch-and-run off the seaside turf at the ninth which finished three feet from the cup, Olazabal reached the turn in 34. On the 12th, he sparked a roar from the crowd when he holed for eagle from 20 yards.

Broader across the shoulders and more powerful than in previous seasons, Olazabal drove the ball well. If his game was in good shape technically, it was also obvious the Spaniard viewed his late qualification as a bonus to be enjoyed while posting rounds of 68, 70, and 68 again to be in second place, two strokes behind.

When he eagled the 18th with a putt from the Valley of Sin on Friday, Olazabal showed his feelings in a manner which echoed Costantino Rocca's famous celebration in 1995. Even though he had spent the first two days in the company of Tiger Woods and his large and excited galleries, an experience

which can leave many drained, the Spaniard said he was at ease in the company of the world's No 1 player.

"I've been more relaxed—nothing

wrong with that," said Olazabal, who was part of the Spanish team which twice won the Dunhill Cup over the Old Course. "I was very relaxed playing with Tiger. I've had three great days on this golf course and I'll try to have as much fun as possible tomorrow. I do have a lot of respect for the golf course, for the tradition and for what it means. Just being able to be part of The Open this year has been wonderful."

—**Mike Aitken**

Thirty-nine years of age at the time, he had been a steady performer over a professional career that had begun in 1985 but been interrupted by a strange condition that affected his toes. After a lengthy series of treatments for rheumatoid arthritis, the wrong ailment, physicians finally found a problem with his lower back. Two joints too close together put pressure on the nerves. Soon he was cured.

Olazabal had been known best for his magical short game, less for his putting, and not at all for his driving, which often enough had left him in unfamiliar territory. For this week, though, his driving had become dependable and his putting

---

Bernhard Langer started with bogeys here at the first and second, then recovered for a two-under 70 round.

In the *Words* of the Competitors...

"

"I hit one bad shot in a fantastic round (drive out of bounds for double-bogey 7 at the 14th). That's the way it goes."

—Soren Hansen

"Today I felt the course was a bit tougher than usual, so it makes the 68 even more satisfying."

—Amateur Lloyd Saltman

"Obviously the whole tournament depends on what Tiger does."

—Darren Clarke

"I did finish well. I made four birdies in the last five holes. I bogeyed the Road Hole. I'm very happy about the way I played."

—Tom Watson

"I played well for 11 holes and poorly for the last seven. If I had played the last seven well, I could have had a chance tomorrow."

—Phil Mickelson

"It's my first time over here. I played with Jack Nicklaus and Tom Watson on Tuesday, and that got me acclimated to the golf course, how they set up the golf course, how they play it."

—Kenny Perry

"

After a bogey here at the Road bunker, Montgomerie recovered for a 70 with a birdie at the last hole.

something special. As an example, he closed out his second round by holing an eagle putt from the Valley of Sin, then, departing from his usual restrained manner, he leaped, and with a yelp shared a high voltage high-five with Woods.

Olly began the day slowly but soundly by playing the opening four holes in par, and then he went to work. A drive and five wood brought him close to the fifth green, but his pitch missed the hole by 30 feet. With new confidence in his putter, Olazabal holed it for his first birdie of the round. Steady play through the eighth, and when his drive didn't reach the ninth green, he played a running shot with his nine iron that stopped within three feet of the hole. Another birdie.

Two under on the outward nine, he played a superb drive to the 12th and holed for an eagle 2 from what he estimated as 20 yards. Now he had climbed to four under par, but it wasn't over just yet. His three wood on the 13th found a bunker and he needed two more to reach the green, setting up his only bogey. He ended with a drive left of the home green, another low running shot on, and a 15-foot putt that fell into the hole.

Olazabal had played the first two rounds alongside Woods, and now he would play the last with him as well.

Round Three Hole Summary

HOLE	PAR	YARDS	EAGLES	BIRDIES	PARS	BOGEYS	D.BOGEYS	HIGHER	RANK	AVERAGE
1	4	376	0	14	57	9	0	0	11	3.94
2	4	453	0	7	59	12	1	1	5	4.13
3	4	397	0	20	52	7	1	0	13	3.86
4	4	480	0	8	59	9	4	0	6	4.11
5	5	568	0	38	32	10	0	0	17	4.65
6	4	412	0	13	57	8	2	0	9	3.99
7	4	390	0	18	52	9	0	1	12	3.93
8	3	175	0	12	60	8	0	0	10	2.95
9	4	352	2	37	29	8	4	0	16	3.69
OUT	**36**	**3603**	**2**	**167**	**457**	**80**	**12**	**2**		**35.24**
10	4	380	0	11	57	11	1	0	8	4.03
11	3	174	0	4	57	18	0	1	3	3.21
12	4	348	1	25	43	8	3	0	15	3.84
13	4	465	0	2	45	31	2	0	2	4.41
14	5	618	0	29	37	10	4	0	13	4.86
15	4	456	0	5	53	22	0	0	3	4.21
16	4	423	0	11	51	16	2	0	6	4.11
17	4	455	0	2	41	30	4	3	1	4.60
18	4	357	2	42	32	4	0	0	18	3.48
IN	**36**	**3676**	**3**	**131**	**416**	**150**	**16**	**4**		**36.75**
TOTAL	**72**	**7279**	**5**	**298**	**873**	**230**	**28**	**6**		**71.99**

Acknowledging the crowd, Woods had just finished a 71 for a two-stroke lead, having two putts for a birdie from 50 yards.

Alone At The Top Again

By Robert Sommers

Tiger Woods demonstrated once again that he was the best player of his time, 75 years after Bobby Jones concluded his career, and two days after Jack Nicklaus ended his, also as the best players of their times.

In one of the more fascinating days of recent Open Championships, Tiger Woods once again forced his dominance on the game with a finishing round of 70 that turned out good enough to increase his margin from two strokes after 54 holes to five strokes at the end, as one after another of his closest challengers closed in but couldn't catch up.

Woods's 72-hole score of 274 fell five strokes behind his winning total of 269 in the 2000 Championship, again over the St Andrews Old Course. Five years earlier he had won by eight strokes.

While Woods displayed his masterly command,

At the 18th, Tiger Woods was left to celebrate.

Colin Montgomerie, spurred on by passionately devoted fans, played the final round in 72 and took second place with 279. Jose Maria Olazabal, who had played his first three rounds in 10 under par, closed with 74 and dropped into a tie for third with the surprising Fred Couples. Forty-five years old in 2005, Couples had crept within sight with a final round of 68 and caught Olazabal, who stumbled through the final nine holes in 39 strokes.

Despite an outcome that had been anticipated, this had been an interesting day nonetheless, as first one man made his move, then another. Spiced by an eagle 3 on the fifth and a birdie 3 on the ninth, Bernhard Langer, for example, played the outward nine in 33 strokes and moved to nine under par. But not for long.

It all ended on the 15th, a tough par-4 of 456 yards. Langer's drive caught the rough and his second shot settled behind a bunker yards short of the green. Then he played a shot with an eight iron that would force a beginner to cringe, which he said was "one of the worst shots I've ever hit." He dumped it into the bunker. With no other option, he played out sideways and walked off with a 6.

Fourth Round Leaders

HOLE	1	2	3	4	5	6	7	8	9	10	11	12	13	14	15	16	17	18	
PAR	4	4	4	4	5	4	4	3	4	4	3	4	4	5	4	4	4	4	TOTAL
Tiger Woods	4	4	4	4	(4)	4	4	3	(3)	[5]	3	(3)	4	(4)	4	4	[5]	4	70-274
Colin Montgomerie	4	4	(3)	4	(4)	4	4	3	(3)	4	[4]	4	[5]	5	4	[5]	4	4	72-279
Fred Couples	(3)	4	4	4	(4)	[5]	4	3	(3)	(3)	3	4	4	5	4	4	4	(3)	68-280
Jose Maria Olazabal	4	4	4	(3)	5	[5]	4	3	(3)	4	3	[5]	[5]	5	[5]	4	[5]	(3)	74-280
Geoff Ogilvy	4	[5]	4	[5]	5	[5]	(3)	3	(3)	4	3	(3)	4	5	(3)	4	(3)	(3)	69-281
Bernhard Langer	4	4	4	4	(3)	4	4	3	(3)	[5]	3	4	4	(4)	[6]	4	[5]	(3)	71-281
Vijay Singh	(3)	4	4	4	5	4	[5]	(2)	4	4	3	(3)	[5]	5	[5]	4	[5]	(3)	72-281
Michael Campbell	4	[5]	4	4	(4)	4	4	3	4	4	3	(3)	4	[6]	4	4	4	4	72-281
Sergio Garcia	4	[5]	4	4	(4)	4	4	3	4	4	3	[6]	[5]	(4)	(3)	4	[5]	(3)	73-281
Retief Goosen	[5]	[5]	4	4	[6]	4	4	[4]	(3)	4	3	[5]	4	(4)	4	4	4	(3)	74-281
Graeme McDowell	4	4	[5]	4	(4)	4	4	3	4	4	3	(3)	(3)	(4)	4	(3)	4	(3)	67-282
Ian Poulter	4	4	(3)	4	5	(3)	4	3	(3)	4	3	4	4	(4)	4	4	[5]	4	69-282
Nick Faldo	4	4	4	4	[6]	4	4	3	(3)	(3)	3	(3)	[5]	[6]	4	4	(3)	(2)	69-282
Kenny Perry	(3)	4	4	[5]	5	4	(3)	[4]	(3)	4	[4]	4	4	5	4	4	4	4	72-282

Nick Faldo was delighted with his birdie on the Road Hole.

Kenny Perry's level-par 72 provided a tie for 11th place.

He finished with 71 and, at 281, tied five others in fifth place.

Then there was Nick Faldo. Not much had been expected of him here, not only because he spent much of his time in television booths, but as well because he would reach age 48 the day after the final round. But then, he had won three Opens, his second in 1990 at St Andrews.

After taking a bogey 5 here on the Road Hole, Sean O'Hair needed a birdie at the 18th for a 73 and a share of 15th place.

Headed for a place among those who tied at 284, Faldo played the last two holes in a total of five strokes—a rare birdie 3 on the Road Hole and an eagle 2 on the last. He turned in his second 69 and a 72-hole score of 282. Had he saved one more stroke he would have caught Michael Campbell, the US Open champion, Retief Goosen, Vijay Singh, Sergio Garcia, Geoff Ogilvy, and Langer, at 281.

While the professionals took most of the glory, Lloyd Saltman, a 19-year-old Scot, played the Old Course in 71 for a total of 283, tied for 15th place, and finished as low amateur among a field of four. He scored one stroke better than Eric Ramsay, another Scot, while the young Italian Edoardo Molinari, who had skipped his graduation ceremonies for The Open, tied for 60th place with 289, and Matthew Richardson, an Englishman, placed last on 297. Still, he had played all 72 holes, quite an accomplishment for an amateur.

No matter the others, this day belonged to Woods. By winning with such command of shots and intelligent tactics, he established himself once again as the best player of his time, just as Jack

Lloyd Saltman got a birdie at the last to win the Silver Medal.

Clockwise from bottom left, Brad Faxon cleared the burn, but his golf ball did not; Sergio Garcia said 'I had my chance' after a 73 left him tied for fifth; Graeme McDowell closed in 67, advancing to the 11th place group.

Nicklaus, who had bowed out earlier in the week, had been the best of his. And he did it 75 years after Bobby Jones had ended his career as the best of *his* time.

With this Championship, Woods had won 10 of golf's most important competitions, known as the four major championships. This was his second Open Championship, he had won two US Opens, two USPGA Championships, and four Masters Tournaments. We might add to those his three successive US Amateur Championships.

His goal, of course, was to exceed Nicklaus's record of 18 professional major titles. By winning this Open Championship, Woods needed eight more. Nicklaus won his 18th at the age of 46, his 10th when he had reached 32. Woods, however, had won The Open 2005 at 29. He would not observe his 30th birthday until late in December. Who dared to guess his final tally?

"It's pretty cool. I've gone one past halfway. Jack's got 18 and I've got 10," Woods said to the press. "Honestly, when I first started playing the Tour, I

Ian Poulter called it 'a frustrating finish' with his bogey on the 17th from the path.

didn't think I would have this many majors before age 30. There's no way. Usually the golden years are in your 30s for a golfer. Hopefully that will be the case."

Woods reminded the press that this was a career opportunity. "It's not going to happen overnight. Jack took 25 years I believe to win all 18 of his," Woods said. "It's going to take a long time to win 18 major championships. More importantly, what did he finish (56 times) in the top five and 19 seconds? There's no other player who has been that consistent in the biggest events.

"To have the opportunity to get to 10 already this soon in my career, it's very exciting to hopefully look forward to some good years in my 30s and hopefully into my 40s."

The road to Woods's 10th had not been without bumps. Entering 2005, he had not won a major title since the US Open of 2002, and he won only one USPGA Tour event in 2004, as he reconstructed a golf swing that, for all anyone but he could see, needed no tampering. But he persisted, and if what he accomplished earlier in 2005 and at St Andrews is the result, it worked.

He of course had already won the 2005 Masters and two other tournaments. By the time he teed off alongside Olazabal just after 2 o'clock in the final Sunday game, Woods had led The Open's last six rounds over the Old Course. Ernie Els had edged him by one stroke after 18 holes five years earlier, but Woods had taken com-

Sunday Weather

Sunny periods with a variable westerly breeze.

Starting three strokes behind, Retief Goosen lost all hope when he went out in 39, then took another bogey here at the 12th.

Memories *of* St Andrews

Martin Kippax
Chairman of Championship
Committee, The R&A

"I've played the Old Course many, many times, but still every time I step onto the first tee, I get the shakes. It's the atmosphere of the course."

mand in the second round and had led from the beginning in 2005. He would be tested, however, over those final 18 holes.

Woods began with a drive to the centre of that wide fairway, a clever tactic that essentially took the Swilcan Burn out of play. That little stream had ruined many a round before it had actually begun. From where his ball lay, Woods approached the green from an angle, played short of the hole onto the left edge of the green where, from this position, his putt would run parallel to the burn, not towards it or possibly into it. Safety first. His ball slipped past the hole, and he began with a routine par 4.

Up ahead, Goosen, a marginal contender at the beginning, pitched well past the hole on the first and three-putted, then pulled his approach to the second into a greenside bunker and bogeyed once again, ending what faint hope he might have had.

After encouraging second and third rounds, Brad Faxon dumped his approach to the first hole into the burn, dropped two strokes, and started with a 6.

Vijay Singh, perpetually on the fringes this week, birdied the first hole but missed birdie putts on the ninth and 10th, scored four 5s over a stretch of five holes on the second nine, only one for a par, scored 72, yet climbed two places into a tie for fifth, at 281.

Round Four Hole Summary

HOLE	PAR	YARDS	EAGLES	BIRDIES	PARS	BOGEYS	D.BOGEYS	HIGHER	RANK	AVERAGE
1	4	376	0	13	53	9	5	0	10	4.08
2	4	453	0	5	51	22	1	1	3	4.28
3	4	397	0	16	59	4	1	0	14	3.88
4	4	480	0	4	56	20	0	0	6	4.20
5	5	568	2	39	35	4	0	0	17	4.51
6	4	412	0	7	54	18	1	0	7	4.16
7	4	390	1	16	54	7	2	0	13	3.91
8	3	175	0	3	63	14	0	0	9	3.14
9	4	352	0	39	32	9	0	0	16	3.63
OUT	**36**	**3603**	**3**	**142**	**457**	**107**	**10**	**1**		**35.78**
10	4	380	0	15	54	11	0	0	12	3.95
11	3	174	0	1	66	12	1	0	7	3.16
12	4	348	0	22	37	18	3	0	11	4.03
13	4	465	0	6	45	27	2	0	2	4.31
14	5	618	0	30	40	8	1	1	15	4.79
15	4	456	0	6	55	15	4	0	4	4.21
16	4	423	0	5	57	15	2	1	4	4.21
17	4	455	0	4	34	34	5	3	1	4.64
18	4	357	2	41	33	4	0	0	18	3.49
IN	**36**	**3676**	**2**	**130**	**421**	**144**	**18**	**5**		**36.79**
TOTAL	**72**	**7279**	**5**	**272**	**878**	**251**	**28**	**6**		**72.57**

Tadahiro Takayama (far left) finished as the leading Japanese player, tied for 23rd place. Geoff Ogilvy (left) was on top of the Australian contingent and shared fifth place.

In the *Words* of the Competitors…

"

"Yesterday was extremely disappointing. I'll have to look and see what the problem is when it comes to majors. I keep throwing in a big number."

—Luke Donald

"There are some courses you feel comfortable on, and this is certainly one of them."

—Tiger Woods

"It's been an amazing finish and I'm very happy that I played well on the last day…. It's been the best experience of my life. It's been good fun."

—Amateur Eric Ramsay

"If you take out the 8 I made on 17 yesterday and I am right back in this golf tournament. It was nice to finish strongly as I did."

—Graeme McDowell

"My game this week was good. I played well. I made a few mistakes. I made a lot of mistakes on the greens. My putter just didn't allow me to be in the golf tournament."

—Tom Watson

"It might be my best finish in a major but I'm not happy. It was a frustrating finish."

—Ian Poulter

"

Round of the **Day**

It wasn't even one of his two lowest scores of the week, but Tiger Woods was extremely pleased with his 70 to win The Open Championship. "It was one of those rounds that I will be thinking about for a long time," Woods said. "I'm very thankful it happened right at the right time."

Woods felt it could be a special day from the time he went to the practice ground. "That was one of the best warm-up sessions I've ever had in my life, right there, this morning," he said. "…And I wanted to carry it to the golf course, and I did."

After playing the first four holes in 4s for pars, Woods posted another 4 for a birdie on the par-5 fifth. He wanted to play the seventh through the 12th in three under par, but instead birdied the par-4 ninth, then bogeyed the par-4 10th after his drive ended in the face of a bunker.

Then came the shot that all but secured the victory. At the same time that Colin Montgomerie and Jose Maria Olazabal were taking bogeys, Woods chipped from the edge of the 12th green to eight feet for a birdie to expand his margin to four strokes. He also birdied the 14th. A bogey on the 17th did not matter.

Faxon, meanwhile, slipped to a closing 76 and tied for 23rd place, at 284.

In the end the Championship would be settled among Woods, Olazabal, who was paired with him, and Montgomerie, playing one hole ahead with Goosen, who was not having a good day. After his two opening bogeys, Retief added another bogey at the fifth for the second straight day, went out in 39, finished with 74, and spent most of his day trying to stay out of Monty's way.

Montgomerie had begun with two routine pars, but after a drive perhaps just 75 yards short of the third green, he pitched on and holed a good putt for a birdie 3. Ten under par now, he had moved within two strokes of Woods. Two holes later he cut the distance to one. His drive on the fifth ran along the heaving ground for some distance before the humps and hollows of this ancient land turned the

Low Scores

Low First Nine
Simon Khan — 31

Low Second Nine
Graeme McDowell — 31

Low Round
Graeme McDowell — 67

Players Below Par	30
Players At Par	10
Players Above Par	40

Woods said, 'I hit the ball so solidly today, all day.'

Bernhard Langer posted a 71 with a double-bogey 6 on 15.

With a level-par 72, Vijay Singh shared fifth place.

ball leftward into the shortest rough. From a playable lie, his iron from about 215 yards ran on, and with a chance for an eagle, his putt skimmed past the hole. He birdied, advanced to 11 under par, and with plenty of holes left, threatened to catch up.

Woods, meanwhile, had played safe, conservative golf and had avoided risks. His pitch to the second, for example, landed closer to the hole of the 16th than the second, but he coaxed his putt within three feet and parred again.

Playing alongside him, Olazabal moved through the first three holes with pars, although he struggled with the second, where he drove into deep rough, hacked out within a few feet of the green, wedged to 18 inches, and saved the 4.

Now he, too, picked up a stroke with a nice pitch to the fourth and a good putt for a birdie 3. Now 11 under, Olly had matched Montgomerie, both of them just one behind.

Woods had thrived on the par-5 holes. He had played the fifth in three under and the 14th in one under—four under in six holes. Now he birdied the fifth once again. Pulling out his driver, he ripped

When Third Place Is Better Than It Appears

When Jose Maria Olazabal holed a 25-foot, big-breaking putt on the final green for a birdie 3, he broke into a huge grin and was both a happy and relieved man. It was not just the fact that he leapt over the six players on seven under with whom he was currently tied, and certainly not the fact that by so doing he won over £100,000 more than he would had he merely two-putted.

It was more the fact that he had tied for third with Fred Couples and that, astonishingly, equalled the best he had ever done in The Open Championship, the major he now most wants to win. Furthermore, his previous third was way back in 1992 at Muirfield, and his overall record in the oldest major—and Olazabal is a great traditionalist—hardly matches the level of his talent.

The Spaniard has played in 20 Opens, but the 2005 version was only the second time he has made the top 10, only the seventh time in the top 20. While his challenge faltered a little in the final round, at least he was in a position to offer one.

Playing with Tiger Woods, and starting two strokes behind him, Olazabal narrowed the difference to one when he birdied the fourth, but that was as close as he was allowed to get. He was still only two behind after 11 holes, but a Tiger birdie and an Olly bogey at the 12th, and the Spaniard was firmly adrift. "It's hard to catch him," Olazabal said. "I don't think it's impossible. But it's close to impossible!"

He was far from discouraged, though. "Three weeks ago," Olazabal said, "if you had told me I would finish third in The Open I would have said you were mad." In those three weeks he tied for eighth in a relatively weak field in the French Open and tied for 25th in the Barclays Scottish Open, and at that point was not even qualified to play in The Open.

By a quirk of fate, not only did Seve Ballesteros pull out because he felt he

Jose Maria Olazabal missed birdie putts here at the seventh and the eighth.

could not justify his place in the tournament, but the man he let in, by virtue of being then the first reserve in the world rankings, was Olazabal.

That may have been lucky, but the Spaniard certainly made the most of it. "I feel it was a very good experience," Olazabal said. "It was a very positive week. I didn't feel any pressure, but it is always difficult to beat Tiger. Maybe I could have played a little better, but I hit three poor drives, at the sixth, the 12th, and the 13th, and they all cost me strokes."

There are times when third place is much better than it looks or sounds, and this was one of them.

—David Davies

Excerpts
FROM THE **Press**

"For the second time in three days, they were standing on roofs and on balconies, hanging out of hotel windows and lining the fairway, 20 even 30 deep, to offer a rapturous reception to a Scottish golfing hero. And that was for the guy finishing second."

—Alan Fraser, *Daily Mail*

"Lloyd Saltman will not receive a brass farthing for his troubles in this year's Open Championship, but securing both the Silver Medal for leading amateur and the respect of those within the professional ranks is more than enough recompense."

—Martin Greig, *The Herald*

"In the end the matador charge did not materialise, but Olazabal at the very least can reflect on a job well done even if he did end the day in slightly worse position than he had begun it."

—Alan Pattullo, *The Scotsman*

"Former Ryder Cup captain Bernhard Langer … had an exciting day and after an eagle on the fifth looked as though he might be able to make an early charge on the leaders. However, he came unstuck on the 14th with a double-bogey 6."

—Matthew Dunn, *Daily Express*

"After losing his dominance for a couple of years while he rebuilt his game, Woods is back stronger and better than ever."

—Oliver Holt, *Daily Mirror*

Saving par here at the ninth, Michael Campbell posted 72 to tie for fifth.

it so far he had nothing left but a seven iron. His first putt ran five feet past, but, calmly, he holed for his first birdie of the day. Woods was two ahead again, for, short of the green with his second, Olazabal had putted his ball on within eight feet but missed. A par 5 and a stroke lost to both Woods and Montgomerie.

The galleries swarmed behind them now, many of them urging Montgomerie, the Scot, to catch up, some pulling for Olazabal, and many more rooting for Woods, who had played such sterling golf through the first three rounds. In his first Open at St Andrews five years earlier, he had bogeyed just three holes, the second hole in the third round and the 17th in both the third and fourth, an incredible record. By now he had lost strokes on five holes, none on the 17th, as one might expect, but two on the 16th, a record obviously not as remarkable as 2000 but certainly impressive.

Truthfully, Montgomerie could have used the gallery's support. Seven times the European Tour's leader in the Order of Merit, he had never won a major championship, and now, at the age of 42, he worried that his time had passed. He had indeed placed second in two US Opens, but in a playoff in 1994 among himself, Loren Roberts, and Ernie Els, who eventually won, Monty played the first nine in 42 strokes. Three years later he finished second to Els once again. He also lost a playoff in the 1995 USPGA Championship to

Colin Montgomerie marched across the Old Course with enthusiastic, flag-waving countrymen cheering him on.

Steve Elkington. He had never placed higher than a tie for eighth in The Open. Now he stood within reach of Woods.

Montgomerie had a routine par on the sixth and a good drive short of Shell bunker on the seventh, but an awful second shot missed the green. Still, he saved his par, added another at the eighth, the first of the two par-3s, then stepped onto the ninth tee.

Here Monty tore into his shot and drove the green, his eagle putt missed but barely, and from three feet he holed for a birdie 3. He had gone out in 33, three under par, and at that stage had gained two strokes on Woods.

Olazabal, though, had not kept up. Eleven under par following his birdie at the fourth, he had failed

Darren Clarke returned a 73 and tied for 15th.

Unflappable Couples Moves Up

After 28 holes of The Open Championship, Fred Couples's thoughts were not of winning but of whether he could complete the round. And if so, in what kind of score? Couples had just struck a shot that completely baffled him, and hurt his back to boot.

"I don't know what happened," Couples said of his tee shot at the short 11th hole that sailed so far right that it carried a huge scoreboard maybe 80 yards off line. "It was a six iron, and although I've seen that sort of thing done before, I've never done it. It wasn't very much fun playing the next four or five holes with an iron because I thought I was going to shank every shot.

"So now," he added, with a grin, "I know what an amateur feels like."

Couples managed a bogey 4 at the 11th, got round in 71, added to his opening 68, to be five under par entering the weekend. "My back kind of gave out, and a lot of swings were not the way you want to swing. But I managed to play well, even if I was a little tired,"

he said. He was also in good humour. "St Andrews is my second favourite (to Augusta National) golf course in the world," he said, and added, about the change made by The R&A in adding new tees, "I think they're phenomenal, I love them."

So saying, Couples went out and played his worst round of the week. Having had only three bogeys in the first 36 holes, he had four in his next 18 holes, and his 73 seemed to drop him out of contention. Not that the unflappable Couples thought of it that way after a fourth round of 68 for a 280 aggregate and a share of third place with Jose Maria Olazabal, six strokes behind.

This was the second time Couples had been third in The Open. He shared third with Mark O'Meara in 1991, three strokes behind Ian Baker-Finch at Royal Birkdale. And this was Couples's third top-10 finish in an Open at St Andrews. He tied for fourth in 1984 and was sixth in 2000.

"It's so much fun to play St Andrews," he said. "It's a unique spot. I've played a lot of Dunhill Cups and Opens here and I really

felt good about going out to play today. The crowds here are fantastic. They know about golf and in a subtle sort of way they root you on. I've always been enamoured by how nice they are, how courteous they are, and how they know how good a shot you have hit."

Couples hit many of those on the closing day. He was never going to catch Tiger Woods—"He's setting the bar so high and he's so strong"—but his four-under-par final-day score moved him impressively up the field.

"I had a great day and it could've been a heck of a lot better," he said. "I birdied the first, lipped out on three, birdied five, and spun out for eagle on the ninth. At 12 (par-4) I drove the green, hit a heck of a putt up the hill to four feet, and missed, and on 14 (par-5) I was pin high right, in an easy spot, and hit a terrible chip.

"With a bit of luck I could've been a couple better."

—David Davies

A birdie at the home hole enabled Fred Couples to return a 68 and join Olazabal in third place, six strokes behind.

Bogeys here at the 12th, then at the 13th, knocked Olazabal out of the race.

to birdie the susceptible fifth, and then made a major mistake on the sixth, not the weakest of the par-4s, but stronger only than the seventh, ninth, 10th, 12th, and 18th, and all but one of those could be driven.

Olly pulled his drive left into one of the Coffins bunkers, which lie between the sixth and 13th fairways. Less than 150 yards from the sixth green, and with his ball in a good lie, he hit his shot heavy. It pulled up short, his pitch fell short as well, and he bogeyed. Over the next three holes, he could have birdied both the seventh and eighth, but his putt on the seventh just slipped past the hole, and on the eighth his ball caught a piece of the hole but refused to fall. His drive stopped short of the ninth green, but a master of the short game, he ran the ball on, made his birdie, and turned for home with

Montgomerie's momentum was halted at the 11th when he took a bogey.

a first-nine score of 35, one under par and 11 under for 63 holes.

While Olazabal had stumbled on the sixth, Woods had played a very long drive. Then, in a stroke of bad luck, his precision pitch flew directly at the hole, hit the flagstick squarely, and bounded 40 or 50 feet back off the green. With his superb short game, Woods ran the ball to five feet and holed the putt for a par that might easily have been a birdie.

One hole later, with his drive sitting in a divot hole, Woods cut his ball out and flew it beyond and left of the hole with so much spin it drew back and almost dived into the hole. But he missed the birdie opening and walked off with a par 4. He missed another on the eighth where his tee shot almost caught the hole for a hole-in-one, but again he missed a makeable putt and parred.

Colin Montgomerie

For A While The Game Was On

Colin Montgomerie was as a stately galleon as he steered a middle-of-the-fairway course down the opening holes. He was three under par on the day for the first nine holes, and after 10 holes, was 12 under par at a point when Woods was 13 under through eight holes. In other words, he had cut Woods's three-shot overnight lead to one. "At that point," said Montgomerie, "it was game on."

Such a state of affairs may have added spice to the Championship, but it was short-lived. When it came to the 11th and the wind switched, the Scot took the wrong club off the tee, a six iron rather than a seven. His ball bounded through the back of the green and he ended up missing from eight feet for his par.

"After that," he said, "I couldn't recapture the momentum I had had over the front half. It threw me a bit."

Woods rolled an eight-footer into the hole for his birdie at the 12th to have the gap between them back at three shots. Then, at almost the same time, Montgomerie widened that gulf to four shots when he missed the green with his six iron at the 13th and took a bogey.

The only time Montgomerie troubled Woods thereafter was at the 17th. As Woods stood over his second, there was a roar from up ahead as the Scot was signing off at the 18th at nine under par. Woods backed off the ball before returning to hit it short of the Road bunker. "The crowd were phenomenal the whole way round," Montgomerie said. "Even when they realised I wasn't going to win, they realised my job in hand was to try to finish second. And they helped me to that cause."

Montgomerie said that he had given everything he had to the day. He had got tantalisingly close to catching Woods, only instead to let him get away again. "My career has been longer than most, and it's nice having a bit of a resurgence now after three years really in the wilderness," he said. "So it's fantastic for me to get back to a position where I was through the '90s in Europe, at least, and there's no disgrace in finishing second to the best player in the world.

"I'm taking away lots of positives this week."

Monty was never going to spend too long worrying about what might have been. Rather was he in the mood to celebrate. "I beat everyone else other than Tiger and this was my best Open finish," he said. His best previous result was a tie for eighth in 1994 at Turnberry. He recalled how his last second place in a major championship had been eight years earlier, when he finished behind Ernie Els in the 1997 US Open. "I'm full of confidence now to know that I'm capable of doing well."

"It's nice that at 42 I can come back and do the same again. What's more," Montgomerie added, "if someone had said to me that I was going to finish second in The Open at St Andrews, I'd have accepted it before we started."

There was more good news for Montgomerie the following morning. In a year which he had started at a lowly 83rd on the world rankings, he had soared to 22nd. His next goal was to get back inside the top 10.

—Lewine Mair

The crowd at the 18th gave Montgomerie a huge ovation.

Championship Totals	
Players Below Par	183
Players At Par	55
Players Above Par	233

Messages For Tiger's Critics And Rivals

Tiger Woods opened a new chapter in the record books here at St Andrews.

By John Hopkins

As the thousands of people made their various ways home from St Andrews, none could have done so with as much satisfaction as Tiger Woods. He had the magnificent Claret Jug in his possession for the second time, having completed his second career sweep of the major championships at St Andrews, where, five years earlier, he had completed his first. Woods, effusive in his praise of Jack Nicklaus, who ended his career in major championships on the Friday, emphasized how evidently he was Nicklaus's successor by winning his 10th professional major, spread-eagling the field to win by five strokes.

At the age of 29, he had become only the third player in history to reach double figures in terms of numbers of professional major victories, behind Nicklaus (18) and Walter Hagen (11). "It's pretty cool. I've gone one past halfway," Woods said. "Honestly, when I first started playing the Tour, I didn't think I would have this many majors before the age of 30. There's no way."

What was better, in this instance, Woods had done it over the Old Course. "To complete my first career Grand Slam and to complete the second at the same place," he said, "that's as special as it gets. The home of golf. This is something you dream about.

"There are some courses you feel comfortable on, and this is certainly one of them. I enjoy the lines here. You hear guys say the lines fit you. The lines certainly do. I may hit bad golf shots, no doubt about it. I did this week. But as far as the look of the golf shot, I feel very comfortable around this golf course. As I've said, I fell in love with it the first time I played it in 1995."

Woods had been only the sixth player in the history of The Open to lead from start to finish. Ted Ray in 1912, Bobby Jones, the amateur, in 1927, Gene Sarazen in 1932, Henry Cotton in 1934, and Tom Weiskopf in 1973 being the others.

All these statistics were as nothing, however, compared to the one that pleased Woods most. Woods had proved his critics wrong. Those who had doubted the wisdom of changing the swing that had won him eight major championships starting with the 1997 Masters and finishing with the 2002 US Open—but then none until the 2005 Masters—were routed and discredited now that Woods had won two of the year's first three major championships and finished second in the third.

It cannot be said with any certainty that on the way home in his private aeroplane on the Sunday night, Woods raised a glass to his newfound success and toasted Hank Haney, the coach with whom he had started working in March 2004 and who had been through so much with Woods. But who could possibly blame him if he had?

"There's never been a time when I thought that I don't need this," Haney said on the evening of his pupil's victory. "All the criticism did was give me and Tiger the motivation to carry on to prove that the changes were going to work. Tiger took what he calls his 'other level' to the course here this week. He has had it on the driving range for some time. Now he is finally trusting it on the course. It was unrelenting at times, but we've taken it and come through the other side. It is time to look forward now, not back."

What Woods had done with Haney's help was nothing less than to start a new chapter in the record books. The five strokes by which he won could have been more. Woods accepted the patriotic gauntlet thrown down by Colin Montgomerie and thousands of fans who wanted to cheer home the Scot, who had been three strokes behind overnight, and by Jose Maria Olazabal, the popular Spaniard who had started the last day only two strokes behind.

For a little over half the last round it was a contest. Then, as quickly as a drive can bound from a firm, fast-running fairway into a bunker, it was over. Montgomerie was gone and so was Olazabal. Woods was able to walk home looking as relaxed as those St Andreans who stroll over the Old Course in the gathering dusk of a summer's evening. Woods was two strokes ahead of Montgomerie on the 11th, three strokes ahead on the 12th, four on the 13th, and five on the 14th.

Of just as much significance as Woods's victory was the message it delivered to his four clear rivals. Everyone thought that Vijay Singh, Phil Mickelson, Ernie Els, and Retief Goosen had closed the gap on Woods during the two years in which Woods went without winning one of the four big prizes in the game. During this time there was talk not of Woods dominating the game again but of being one of the five men who would scrap for the sport's greatest prizes on a more equal footing.

So much for that. With his performance over the Old Course, Woods rendered such talk fanciful. If there was one other thing it is certain that Woods thought about as he flew home, it is that he had done a very good job of sowing seeds of self-doubt into the minds of his four rivals. If these four men, the youngest of whom, Mickelson, is six years older and the oldest, Singh, 13, do not have the will or the heart to renew their efforts, then their challenge to Woods will be diminished by each passing month. They have to start all over again or watch Woods move further ahead.

This then was the most noticeable aspect of Woods's triumph at St Andrews. It was not the length he hit the ball, though that was considerable. It was not the way he managed his game nor the skill with which he played nor the repetitive nature of his swing. It was the way he put his spiked golf shoes on the throats of his rivals. Not a pleasant thought for spectators to consider, but a far worse feeling for Singh, Mickelson, Goosen, and Els.

The decisive shots were on the 12th, where Woods chipped to eight feet for a birdie.

On to the ninth, a hole that had been especially kind to him. He had birdied twice, his only 4 following a drive the previous day that scooted into the gorse and cost him a penalty stroke. Here though, he played another massive drive that for a scary moment looked as if it might dive into End bunker. Instead it cleared the hazard nicely, settled on the green, and he two-putted for another birdie.

Woods had gone out in 34, gained one stroke on Olazabal, dropping him three strokes behind, but lost one to Montgomerie, one hole ahead and two strokes behind. Within the next three holes, the Championship changed.

"Sunday brought yet another grand crossing over the Swilcan Bridge. The defiant return of Tiger Woods."
—**Doug Ferguson, The Associated Press**

"So many hopes, so many dreams, so much emotion, but just one glaring reality. His name was Tiger Woods. He won The Open Championship by five shots. And he didn't even play that well. That was the spookily familiar truth that the world of golf will have to come to terms with once more."
—**James Corrigan, *The Independent***

"His pursuers had vanished from the fight, leaving Tiger Woods alone to stride … toward the Claret Jug he had been waiting all week to claim."
—**Damon Hack, *The New York Times***

"In the end, it all fit together more perfectly than golf, Guinness, and gorse."
—**Glenn Sheeley, *Atlanta Journal-Constitution***

"For all nine years of his professional life, Tiger Woods has managed to hold the world at large at arm's length. So maintaining a discreet distance between himself, Colin Montgomerie, Jose Maria Olazabal, and the rest of The Open Championship field proved a stroll."
—**Mike Selvey, *The Guardian***

"The greatest frontrunner golf has ever known did it again."
—**Mark Garrod, Press Association**

With his followers waving Scottish flags, Montgomerie parred the 10th, then once again overshot the 11th, a difficult par-3 with a green that rises sharply towards the back. He faced a scary chip that, besides its speed, called for a substantial right-to-left break. Monty played it nicely, but it turned too soon and left him with too much work to do. He bogeyed.

The error cost him dearly, for just then Woods dropped a stroke on the 10th, one of those holes he practically owned. He had played the 10th in two under par, but now he gave away a stroke, a sin he so seldom committed this week.

Evidently going for the green with his driver on a hole that measured 380 yards—remember, he had driven it earlier—he caught a solitary bunker within about 50 yards of safety. It was a small bunker, but his ball lay so close to the front wall

A thumbs-up from the champion.

he could do nothing but play back towards the tee. From there he putted his ball onto the green, then missed from about 10 feet. One stroke gone, but instead of showing anger, Woods walked away with a sheepish smile, embarrassed perhaps by his ridiculous manner of playing the hole.

Moving on to the 11th tee, Woods played a nice eight iron inside 20 feet and got down in two for the par, then stepped onto the 12th tee.

The next few minutes settled The Open.

Woods drove into the left rough close to the green, chipped to within holing distance, eight feet, read the break precisely, and holed the putt for a birdie 3. Now he stood 14 under par. Olazabal, though, bogeyed and fell four behind.

Montgomerie, meanwhile, two behind as he stood on the 13th tee, drove with an iron and with his

next shot went for the green with a six iron. His ball hung up in the wind and fell short. He played a little flip shot to five feet, but he missed the putt for a bogey 5 and a two-stroke swing. Monty had fallen four strokes behind Woods as well.

It was over. Neither Montgomerie nor Olazabal could hope to catch Woods now, and of course they didn't. From here in Woods need do nothing more than run up the pars, avoid careless mistakes, and claim the trophy.

On and on he went. A big drive on the 14th led to another birdie and now he led by five strokes. That is how it ended.

Woods played the 17th cautiously and deliberately played for a 5 rather than risk something worse. One more hole and he could safely tuck away yet another Championship.

As he stepped onto the 18th tee, the volume of the gallery's applause rose to its crescendo. As is customary, spectators crammed the big grandstands beside and behind the double fairway and lined the road running alongside. Others leaned out windows in privates houses, watched from the windows of the St Andrews Golf Club, crowded balconies of Rusacks and Forgan House, and some daring souls climbed to rooftops for a glimpse of this young man who had won this, the oldest Championship in golf, so completely and decisively.

He played the 18th with great caution. Dismissing any chance of driving either out of bounds or leaving himself an awkward approach, he drove with an iron that left him well short of the green, ran his approach short, rolled the ball on with his third, and holed his putt for a safe par 4.

He had come back in 36, and with his closing 70, won by a decisive five strokes.

Championship Hole Summary

HOLE	PAR	YARDS	EAGLES	BIRDIES	PARS	BOGEYS	D.BOGEYS	HIGHER	RANK	AVERAGE
1	4	376	0	87	323	48	13	0	12	3.97
2	4	453	0	46	294	113	11	7	4	4.24
3	4	397	0	103	328	38	2	0	14	3.87
4	4	480	0	27	309	118	14	3	3	4.27
5	5	568	15	211	191	46	6	2	17	4.62
6	4	412	0	56	334	74	7	0	9	4.07
7	4	390	1	85	322	52	8	3	11	3.98
8	3	175	0	39	345	85	2	0	8	3.11
9	4	352	9	212	196	48	6	0	16	3.64
OUT	**36**	**3603**	**25**	**866**	**2642**	**622**	**69**	**15**		**35.77**
10	4	380	0	78	336	53	4	0	13	3.96
11	3	174	0	34	321	107	6	3	5	3.20
12	4	348	2	105	272	81	9	2	10	3.99
13	4	465	0	19	271	158	23	0	2	4.39
14	5	618	3	168	214	69	14	3	15	4.86
15	4	456	0	48	318	96	7	2	7	4.14
16	4	423	0	34	332	90	12	3	6	4.19
17	4	455	0	19	217	182	33	20	1	4.63
18	4	357	9	220	223	17	2	0	18	3.54
IN	**36**	**3676**	**14**	**725**	**2504**	**853**	**110**	**33**		**36.91**
TOTAL	**72**	**7279**	**39**	**1591**	**5146**	**1475**	**179**	**48**		**72.68**

Woods followed Jack Nicklaus on the 18th by almost exactly 48 hours.

It's a Fact

With 13 major championships—10 professional and three US Amateur titles—Tiger Woods has matched the total of Bobby Jones, second behind Jack Nicklaus's record of 20. Jones completed his total and retired in 1930 at the age of 28, one year younger than Woods is now. Nicklaus won his 10th major championship (including two in the US Amateur) in the 1970 Open at St Andrews (at age 30) and his 10th professional major in the 1972 Masters (at age 32).

There is always
a special flavour
to the finish
of Thc Open
Championship.

The Open Championship Results

Year	Champion	Score	Margin	Runners-up	Venue
1860	Willie Park Snr	174	2	Tom Morris Snr	Prestwick
1861	Tom Morris Snr	163	4	Willie Park Snr	Prestwick
1862	Tom Morris Snr	163	13	Willie Park Snr	Prestwick
1863	Willie Park Snr	168	2	Tom Morris Snr	Prestwick
1864	Tom Morris Snr	167	2	Andrew Strath	Prestwick
1865	Andrew Strath	162	2	Willie Park Snr	Prestwick
1866	Willie Park Snr	169	2	David Park	Prestwick
1867	Tom Morris Snr	170	2	Willie Park Snr	Prestwick
1868	Tom Morris Jnr	154	3	Tom Morris Snr	Prestwick
1869	Tom Morris Jnr	157	11	Bob Kirk	Prestwick
1870	Tom Morris Jnr	149	12	Bob Kirk, David Strath	Prestwick
1871	*No Competition*				
1872	Tom Morris Jnr	166	3	David Strath	Prestwick
1873	Tom Kidd	179	1	Jamie Anderson	St Andrews
1874	Mungo Park	159	2	Tom Morris Jnr	Musselburgh
1875	Willie Park Snr	166	2	Bob Martin	Prestwick
1876	Bob Martin	176	—	David Strath	St Andrews
	(Martin was awarded the title when Strath refused to play-off)				
1877	Jamie Anderson	160	2	Bob Pringle	Musselburgh
1878	Jamie Anderson	157	2	Bob Kirk	Prestwick
1879	Jamie Anderson	169	3	James Allan, Andrew Kirkaldy	St Andrews
1880	Bob Ferguson	162	5	Peter Paxton	Musselburgh
1881	Bob Ferguson	170	3	Jamie Anderson	Prestwick
1882	Bob Ferguson	171	3	Willie Fernie	St Andrews
1883	Willie Fernie	158	Playoff	Bob Ferguson	Musselburgh
1884	Jack Simpson	160	4	Douglas Rolland, Willie Fernie	Prestwick
1885	Bob Martin	171	1	Archie Simpson	St Andrews
1886	David Brown	157	2	Willie Campbell	Musselburgh
1887	Willie Park Jnr	161	1	Bob Martin	Prestwick
1888	Jack Burns	171	1	David Anderson Jnr, Ben Sayers	St Andrews
1889	Willie Park Jnr	155	Playoff	Andrew Kirkaldy	Musselburgh
1890	*John Ball Jnr	164	3	Willie Fernie, Archie Simpson	Prestwick
1891	Hugh Kirkaldy	166	2	Willie Fernie, Andrew Kirkaldy	St Andrews

(From 1892 the competition was extended to 72 holes)

Year	Champion	Score	Margin	Runners-up	Venue
1892	*Harold Hilton	305	3	*John Ball Jnr, Hugh Kirkaldy, Sandy Herd	Muirfield

Year	Champion	Score	Margin	Runners-up	Venue
1893	Willie Auchterlonie	322	2	*John Laidlay	Prestwick
1894	J.H. Taylor	326	5	Douglas Rolland	Sandwich
1895	J.H. Taylor	322	4	Sandy Herd	St Andrews
1896	Harry Vardon	316	Playoff	J.H. Taylor	Muirfield
1897	*Harold Hilton	314	1	James Braid	Hoylake
1898	Harry Vardon	307	1	Willie Park Jnr	Prestwick
1899	Harry Vardon	310	5	Jack White	Sandwich
1900	J.H. Taylor	309	8	Harry Vardon	St Andrews
1901	James Braid	309	3	Harry Vardon	Muirfield
1902	Sandy Herd	307	1	Harry Vardon, James Braid	Hoylake
1903	Harry Vardon	300	6	Tom Vardon	Prestwick
1904	Jack White	296	1	James Braid, J.H. Taylor	Sandwich
1905	James Braid	318	5	J.H. Taylor, Rowland Jones	St Andrews
1906	James Braid	300	4	J.H. Taylor	Muirfield
1907	Arnaud Massy	312	2	J.H. Taylor	Hoylake
1908	James Braid	291	8	Tom Ball	Prestwick
1909	J.H. Taylor	295	6	James Braid, Tom Ball	Deal
1910	James Braid	299	4	Sandy Herd	St Andrews
1911	Harry Vardon	303	Playoff	Arnaud Massy	Sandwich
1912	Ted Ray	295	4	Harry Vardon	Muirfield
1913	J.H. Taylor	304	8	Ted Ray	Hoylake
1914	Harry Vardon	306	3	J.H. Taylor	Prestwick
1915-1919	No Championship				
1920	George Duncan	303	2	Sandy Herd	Deal
1921	Jock Hutchison	296	Playoff	*Roger Wethered	St Andrews
1922	Walter Hagen	300	1	George Duncan, Jim Barnes	Sandwich
1923	Arthur G. Havers	295	1	Walter Hagen	Troon
1924	Walter Hagen	301	1	Ernest Whitcombe	Hoylake
1925	Jim Barnes	300	1	Archie Compston, Ted Ray	Prestwick
1926	*Robert T. Jones Jnr	291	2	Al Watrous	Royal Lytham
1927	*Robert T. Jones Jnr	285	6	Aubrey Boomer, Fred Robson	St Andrews
1928	Walter Hagen	292	2	Gene Sarazen	Sandwich
1929	Walter Hagen	292	6	John Farrell	Muirfield
1930	*Robert T. Jones Jnr	291	2	Leo Diegel, Macdonald Smith	Hoylake

Tony Jacklin (1969)

Tom Watson (1975, 1977, 1980, 1982, 1983)

Jack Nicklaus (1966, 1970, 1978)

Year	Champion	Score	Margin	Runners-up	Venue
1931	Tommy Armour	296	1	Jose Jurado	Carnoustie
1932	Gene Sarazen	283	5	Macdonald Smith	Prince's
1933	Densmore Shute	292	Playoff	Craig Wood	St Andrews
1934	Henry Cotton	283	5	Sid Brews	Sandwich
1935	Alf Perry	283	4	Alf Padgham	Muirfield
1936	Alf Padgham	287	1	Jimmy Adams	Hoylake
1937	Henry Cotton	290	2	Reg Whitcombe	Carnoustie
1938	Reg Whitcombe	295	2	Jimmy Adams	Sandwich
1939	Richard Burton	290	2	Johnny Bulla	St Andrews
1940-1945 No Championship					
1946	Sam Snead	290	4	Bobby Locke, Johnny Bulla	St Andrews
1947	Fred Daly	293	1	Reg Horne, *Frank Stranahan	Hoylake
1948	Henry Cotton	284	5	Fred Daly	Muirfield
1949	Bobby Locke	283	Playoff	Harry Bradshaw	Sandwich
1950	Bobby Locke	279	2	Roberto de Vicenzo	Troon
1951	Max Faulkner	285	2	Tony Cerda	Royal Portrush
1952	Bobby Locke	287	1	Peter Thomson	Royal Lytham
1953	Ben Hogan	282	4	*Frank Stranahan, Dai Rees, Peter Thomson, Tony Cerda	Carnoustie
1954	Peter Thomson	283	1	Sid Scott, Dai Rees, Bobby Locke	Royal Birkdale
1955	Peter Thomson	281	2	Johnny Fallon	St Andrews
1956	Peter Thomson	286	3	Flory van Donck	Hoylake
1957	Bobby Locke	279	3	Peter Thomson	St Andrews
1958	Peter Thomson	278	Playoff	David Thomas	Royal Lytham
1959	Gary Player	284	2	Flory van Donck, Fred Bullock	Muirfield
1960	Kel Nagle	278	1	Arnold Palmer	St Andrews
1961	Arnold Palmer	284	1	Dai Rees	Royal Birkdale
1962	Arnold Palmer	276	6	Kel Nagle	Troon
1963	Bob Charles	277	Playoff	Phil Rodgers	Royal Lytham
1964	Tony Lema	279	5	Jack Nicklaus	St Andrews
1965	Peter Thomson	285	2	Christy O'Connor, Brian Huggett	Royal Birkdale
1966	Jack Nicklaus	282	1	David Thomas, Doug Sanders	Muirfield
1967	Roberto de Vicenzo	278	2	Jack Nicklaus	Hoylake
1968	Gary Player	289	2	Jack Nicklaus, Bob Charles	Carnoustie
1969	Tony Jacklin	280	2	Bob Charles	Royal Lytham
1970	Jack Nicklaus	283	Playoff	Doug Sanders	St Andrews

Mark Calcavecchia (1989)

Mark O'Meara (1998)

Tom Lehman (1996)

Nick Price (1994)

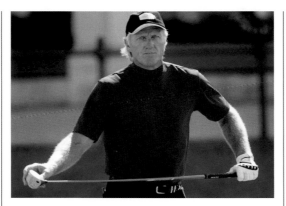

Greg Norman (1986, 1993)

Nick Faldo (1987, 1990, 1992)

Year	Champion	Score	Margin	Runners-up	Venue
1971	Lee Trevino	278	1	Lu Liang Huan	Royal Birkdale
1972	Lee Trevino	278	1	Jack Nicklaus	Muirfield
1973	Tom Weiskopf	276	3	Neil Coles, Johnny Miller	Troon
1974	Gary Player	282	4	Peter Oosterhuis	Royal Lytham
1975	Tom Watson	279	Playoff	Jack Newton	Carnoustie
1976	Johnny Miller	279	6	Jack Nicklaus, Severiano Ballesteros	Royal Birkdale
1977	Tom Watson	268	1	Jack Nicklaus	Turnberry
1978	Jack Nicklaus	281	2	Simon Owen, Ben Crenshaw, Raymond Floyd, Tom Kite	St Andrews
1979	Severiano Ballesteros	283	3	Jack Nicklaus, Ben Crenshaw	Royal Lytham
1980	Tom Watson	271	4	Lee Trevino	Muirfield
1981	Bill Rogers	276	4	Bernhard Langer	Sandwich
1982	Tom Watson	284	1	Peter Oosterhuis, Nick Price	Royal Troon
1983	Tom Watson	275	1	Hale Irwin, Andy Bean	Royal Birkdale
1984	Severiano Ballesteros	276	2	Bernhard Langer, Tom Watson	St Andrews
1985	Sandy Lyle	282	1	Payne Stewart	Sandwich
1986	Greg Norman	280	5	Gordon J. Brand	Turnberry
1987	Nick Faldo	279	1	Rodger Davis, Paul Azinger	Muirfield
1988	Severiano Ballesteros	273	2	Nick Price	Royal Lytham
1989	Mark Calcavecchia	275	Playoff	Greg Norman, Wayne Grady	Royal Troon
1990	Nick Faldo	270	5	Mark McNulty, Payne Stewart	St Andrews
1991	Ian Baker-Finch	272	2	Mike Harwood	Royal Birkdale
1992	Nick Faldo	272	1	John Cook	Muirfield
1993	Greg Norman	267	2	Nick Faldo	Sandwich
1994	Nick Price	268	1	Jesper Parnevik	Turnberry
1995	John Daly	282	Playoff	Costantino Rocca	St Andrews
1996	Tom Lehman	271	2	Mark McCumber, Ernie Els	Royal Lytham
1997	Justin Leonard	272	3	Jesper Parnevik, Darren Clarke	Royal Troon
1998	Mark O'Meara	280	Playoff	Brian Watts	Royal Birkdale
1999	Paul Lawrie	290	Playoff	Justin Leonard, Jean Van de Velde	Carnoustie
2000	Tiger Woods	269	8	Ernie Els, Thomas Bjorn	St Andrews
2001	David Duval	274	3	Niclas Fasth	Royal Lytham
2002	Ernie Els	278	Playoff	Thomas Levet, Stuart Appleby, Steve Elkington	Muirfield
2003	Ben Curtis	283	1	Thomas Bjorn, Vijay Singh	Sandwich
2004	Todd Hamilton	274	Playoff	Ernie Els	Royal Troon
2005	Tiger Woods	274	5	Colin Montgomerie	St Andrews

*Denotes amateurs

The Open Championship Records

Most Victories

6, Harry Vardon, 1896-98-99-1903-11-14
5, James Braid, 1901-05-06-08-10; J.H. Taylor, 1894-95-1900-09-13; Peter Thomson, 1954-55-56-58-65; Tom Watson, 1975-77-80-82-83

Most Times Runner-Up or Joint Runner-Up

7, Jack Nicklaus, 1964-67-68-72-76-77-79
6, J.H. Taylor, 1896-1904-05-06-07-14

Oldest Winner

Old Tom Morris, 46 years 99 days, 1867
Harry Vardon, 44 years 41 days, 1914
Roberto de Vicenzo, 44 years 93 days, 1967

Youngest Winner

*Young Tom Morris, 17 years 5 months 8 days, 1868
Willie Auchterlonie, 21 years 24 days, 1893
Severiano Ballesteros, 22 years 3 months 12 days, 1979

Youngest and Oldest Competitor

*Young Tom Morris, 14 years 4 months 4 days, 1865
Gene Sarazen, 74 years 4 months 9 days, 1976
*From date of christening; date of birth not known.

Biggest Margin of Victory

13 strokes, Old Tom Morris, 1862
12 strokes, Young Tom Morris, 1870
11 strokes, Young Tom Morris, 1869
8 strokes, J.H. Taylor, 1900 and 1913; James Braid, 1908; Tiger Woods, 2000

Lowest Winning Aggregates

267 (66, 68, 69, 64), Greg Norman, Royal St George's, 1993
268 (68, 70, 65, 65), Tom Watson, Turnberry, 1977; (69, 66, 67, 66), Nick Price, Turnberry, 1994
269 (67, 66, 67, 69), Tiger Woods, St Andrews, 2000

Lowest Aggregates in Relation to Par

269 (19 under par), Tiger Woods, St Andrews, 2000
270 (18 under par), Nick Faldo, St Andrews, 1990

Lowest Aggregates by Runner-Up

269 (68, 70, 65, 66), Jack Nicklaus, Turnberry, 1977; (69, 63, 70, 67), Nick Faldo, Royal St George's, 1993; (68, 66, 68, 67), Jesper Parnevik, Turnberry, 1994

Lowest Aggregates by an Amateur

281 (68, 72, 70, 71), Iain Pyman, Royal St George's, 1993; (75, 66, 70, 70), Tiger Woods, Royal Lytham, 1996

Lowest Individual Round

63, Mark Hayes, second round, Turnberry, 1977; Isao Aoki, third round, Muirfield, 1980; Greg Norman, second round, Turnberry, 1986; Paul Broadhurst, third round, St Andrews, 1990; Jodie Mudd, fourth round, Royal Birkdale, 1991; Nick Faldo, second round, and Payne Stewart, fourth round, Royal St George's, 1993

Lowest Individual Round by an Amateur

66, Frank Stranahan, fourth round, Troon, 1950; Tiger Woods, second round, Royal Lytham, 1996; Justin Rose, second round, Royal Birkdale, 1998

Tiger Woods (2000, 2005)

Past champions, first row (from left) **Bob Charles, Greg Norman, Nick Faldo, Jack Nicklaus, Peter Thomson, Richard Cole-Hamilton (Captain of The Royal and Ancient Golf Club), Todd Hamilton, Tom Watson, Gary Player, Seve Ballesteros, Nick Price.** Second row, **Tom Lehman, Mark O'Meara, Ben Curtis, Sandy Lyle, Tony Jacklin, Ernie Els, Ian Baker-Finch, Mark Calcavecchia, Paul Lawrie, Tiger Woods, David Duval, Justin Leonard.**

Lowest First Round

64, Craig Stadler, Royal Birkdale, 1983; Christy O'Connor Jnr., Royal St George's, 1985; Rodger Davis, Muirfield, 1987; Raymond Floyd and Steve Pate, Muirfield, 1992

Lowest Second Round

63, Mark Hayes, Turnberry, 1977; Greg Norman, Turnberry, 1986; Nick Faldo, Royal St George's, 1993

Lowest Third Round

63, Isao Aoki, Muirfield, 1980; Paul Broadhurst, St Andrews, 1990

Lowest Fourth Round

63, Jodie Mudd, Royal Birkdale, 1991; Payne Stewart, Royal St George's, 1993

Lowest First 36 Holes

130 (66, 64), Nick Faldo, Muirfield, 1992

Lowest Second 36 Holes

130 (65, 65), Tom Watson, Turnberry, 1977; (64, 66), Ian Baker-Finch, Royal Birkdale, 1991; (66, 64), Anders Forsbrand, Turnberry, 1994

Lowest Middle 36 Holes

130 (66, 64), Fuzzy Zoeller, Turnberry, 1994

Lowest First 54 Holes

198 (67, 67, 64), Tom Lehman, Royal Lytham, 1996
199 (67, 65, 67), Nick Faldo, St Andrews, 1990; (66, 64, 69), Nick Faldo, Muirfield, 1992

Lowest Final 54 Holes

199 (66, 67, 66), Nick Price, Turnberry, 1994

Lowest 9 Holes

28, Denis Durnian, first 9, Royal Birkdale, 1983
29, Peter Thomson and Tom Haliburton, first 9, Royal Lytham, 1958; Tony Jacklin, first 9, St Andrews, 1970; Bill Longmuir, first 9, Royal Lytham, 1979; David J. Russell, first 9, Royal Lytham, 1988; Ian Baker-Finch and Paul Broadhurst, first 9, St Andrews, 1990; Ian Baker-Finch, first 9, Royal Birkdale, 1991; Paul McGinley, first 9, Royal Lytham, 1996; Ernie Els, first 9, Muirfield, 2002

Successive Victories

4, Young Tom Morris, 1868-72 (no Championship in 1871).
3, Jamie Anderson, 1877-79; Bob Ferguson, 1880-82, Peter Thomson, 1954-56
2, Old Tom Morris, 1861-62; J.H. Taylor, 1894-95; Harry Vardon, 1898-99; James Braid, 1905-06; Bobby Jones, 1926-27; Walter Hagen, 1928-29; Bobby Locke, 1949-50; Arnold Palmer, 1961-62; Lee Trevino, 1971-72; Tom Watson, 1982-83

Victories by Amateurs

3, Bobby Jones, 1926-27-30
2, Harold Hilton, 1892-97
1, John Ball, 1890
Roger Wethered lost a playoff in 1921

Champions in First Appearance

Willie Park, Prestwick, 1860; Tom Kidd, St Andrews, 1873; Mungo Park, Musselburgh, 1874; Harold Hilton, Muirfield, 1892; Jock Hutchison, St Andrews, 1921; Densmore Shute, St Andrews, 1933; Ben Hogan, Carnoustie, 1953; Tony Lema, St Andrews, 1964; Tom Watson, Carnoustie, 1975; Ben Curtis, Sandwich, 2003

Biggest Span Between First and Last Victories

19 years, J.H. Taylor, 1894-1913
18 years, Harry Vardon, 1896-1914
15 years, Gary Player, 1959-74
14 years, Willie Park Snr, 1860-75 (no competition 1871); Henry Cotton, 1934-48

Biggest Span Between Victories

11 years, Henry Cotton, 1937-48

Champions in Three Decades

Harry Vardon, 1896, 1903, 1911
J.H. Taylor, 1894, 1900, 1913
Gary Player, 1959, 1968, 1974

Ernie Els (2002)

John Daly (1995)

David Duval (2001)

Highest Number of Top-Five Finishes

16, J.H. Taylor, Jack Nicklaus
15, Harry Vardon, James Braid

Highest Number of Rounds Under Par

61, Jack Nicklaus
52, Nick Faldo
42, Tom Watson

Highest Number of Aggregates Under Par

14, Jack Nicklaus, Nick Faldo

Most Consecutive Rounds Under 70

7, Ernie Els, 1993-94

Outright Leader After Every Round

Ted Ray, 1912; Bobby Jones, 1927; Gene Sarazen, 1932; Henry Cotton, 1934; Tom Weiskopf, 1973; Tiger Woods, 2005

Leader After Every Round Including Ties

Harry Vardon, 1899 and 1903; J.H. Taylor, 1900; Lee Trevino, 1971; Gary Player, 1974

Record Leads (Since 1892)

After 18 holes:
4 strokes, James Braid, 1908; Bobby Jones, 1927; Henry Cotton, 1934; Christy O'Connor Jnr., 1985
After 36 holes:
9 strokes, Henry Cotton, 1934
After 54 holes:
10 strokes, Henry Cotton, 1934
7 strokes, Tony Lema, 1964

Biggest Leads by Non-Champions

After 54 holes:
5 strokes, Macdonald Smith, 1925; Jean Van de Velde, 1999

Champions with Each Round Lower Than Previous One

Jack White, 1904, Sandwich, (80, 75, 72, 69)
James Braid, 1906, Muirfield, (77, 76, 74, 73)
Henry Cotton, 1937, Carnoustie, (74, 73, 72, 71)
Ben Hogan, 1953, Carnoustie, (73, 71, 70, 68)
Gary Player, 1959, Muirfield, (75, 71, 70, 68)

Champion with Four Rounds the Same

Densmore Shute, 1933, St Andrews, (73, 73, 73, 73) (excluding the playoff)

Biggest Variation Between Rounds of a Champion

14 strokes, Henry Cotton, 1934, second round 65, fourth round 79
11 strokes, Jack White, 1904, first round 80, fourth round 69; Greg Norman, 1986, first round 74, second round 63, third round 74

Justin Leonard (1997)

Paul Lawrie (1999)

Ben Curtis (2003)

Todd Hamilton (2004)

Biggest Variation Between Two Rounds

20 strokes, R.G. French, 1938, second round 71, third round 91; Colin Montgomerie, 2002, second round 64, third round 84
19 strokes, R.H. Pemberton, 1938, second round 72, third round 91
18 strokes, A. Tingey Jnr., 1923, first round 94, second round 76
17 strokes, Jack Nicklaus, 1981, first round 83, second round 66; Ian Baker-Finch, 1986, first round 86, second round 69

Best Comeback by Champions

After 18 holes:
Harry Vardon, 1896, 11 strokes behind the leader
After 36 holes:
George Duncan, 1920, 13 strokes behind the leader
After 54 holes:
Paul Lawrie, 1999, 10 strokes behind the leader

Champions with Four Rounds Under 70

Greg Norman, 1993, Royal St George's, (66, 68, 69, 64); Nick Price, 1994, Turnberry, (69, 66, 67, 66); Tiger Woods, 2000, St Andrews, (67, 66, 67, 69)
Of non-champions:
Ernie Els, 1993, Royal St George's, (68, 69, 69, 68); Jesper Parnevik, 1994, Turnberry, (68, 66, 68, 67); Ernie Els, 2004, Royal Troon, (69, 69, 68, 68)

Best Finishing Round by a Champion

64, Greg Norman, Royal St George's, 1993
65, Tom Watson, Turnberry, 1977; Severiano Ballesteros, Royal Lytham, 1988; Justin Leonard, Royal Troon, 1997

Worst Round by a Champion Since 1939

78, Fred Daly, third round, Hoylake, 1947
76, Paul Lawrie, third round, Carnoustie, 1999

Worst Finishing Round by a Champion Since 1939

75, Sam Snead, St Andrews, 1946

Best Opening Round by a Champion

66, Peter Thomson, Royal Lytham, 1958; Nick Faldo, Muirfield, 1992; Greg Norman, Royal St George's, 1993; Tiger Woods, St Andrews, 2005

Biggest Recovery in 18 Holes by a Champion

George Duncan, Deal, 1920, was 13 strokes behind the leader, Abe Mitchell, after 36 holes and level after 54

Most Appearances

46, Gary Player
38, Jack Nicklaus

Most Appearances on Final Day (Since 1892)

32, Jack Nicklaus
31, Alex Herd
30, J.H. Taylor
27, Harry Vardon, James Braid, Nick Faldo
26, Peter Thomson, Gary Player
23, Dai Rees
22, Henry Cotton

Most Appearances Before First Victory

16, Nick Price, 1994
14, Mark O'Meara, 1998

Most Appearances Without a Victory

29, Dai Rees
28, Sam Torrance
27, Neil Coles

Championship with Highest Number of Rounds Under 70

148, Turnberry, 1994

Championship Since 1946 with the Fewest Rounds Under 70

St Andrews, 1946; Hoylake, 1947; Portrush, 1951; Hoylake, 1956; Carnoustie, 1968. All had only two rounds under 70.

Longest Course

Carnoustie, 1999, 7361 yards

Courses Most Often Used

St Andrews, 27; Prestwick, 24; Muirfield, 15; Sandwich, 13; Hoylake and Royal Lytham, 10; Royal Birkdale and Royal Troon, 8; Musselburgh and Carnoustie, 6; Turnberry, 3; Deal, 2; Royal Portrush and Prince's, 1

Prize Money

Year	Total	First Prize
1860	nil	nil
1863	10	nil
1864	15	6
1876	27	10
1889	22	8
1891	30.50	10
1892	100	35
1893	100	30
1910	135	50
1920	225	75
1927	275	75
1930	400	100
1931	500	100
1946	1,000	150
1949	1,500	300
1953	2,500	500
1954	3,500	750
1955	3,750	1,000
1958	4,850	1,000
1959	5,000	1,000
1960	7,000	1,250
1961	8,500	1,400
1963	8,500	1,500
1965	10,000	1,750
1966	15,000	2,100
1968	20,000	3,000
1969	30,334	4,250
1970	40,000	5,250
1971	45,000	5,500
1972	50,000	5,500
1975	75,000	7,500
1977	100,000	10,000
1978	125,000	12,500
1979	155,000	15,000
1980	200,000	25,000
1982	250,000	32,000
1983	310,000	40,000
1984	445,000	50,000
1985	530,000	65,000
1986	634,000	70,000
1987	650,000	75,000
1988	700,000	80,000
1989	750,000	80,000
1990	825,000	85,000

Year	Total	First Prize
1991	900,000	90,000
1992	950,000	95,000
1993	1,000,000	100,000
1994	1,100,000	110,000
1995	1,250,000	125,000
1996	1,400,000	200,000
1997	1,586,300	250,000
1998	1,800,000	300,000

Year	Total	First Prize
1999	2,000,000	350,000
2000	2,750,000	500,000
2001	3,300,000	600,000
2002	3,800,000	700,000
2003	3,900,000	700,000
2004	4,000,000	720,000
2005	4,000,000	720,000

Attendance

Year	Total
1962	37,098
1963	24,585
1964	35,954
1965	32,927
1966	40,182
1967	29,880
1968	51,819
1969	46,001
1970	81,593
1971	70,076
1972	84,746
1973	78,810
1974	92,796
1975	85,258
1976	92,021

Year	Total
1977	87,615
1978	125,271
1979	134,501
1980	131,610
1981	111,987
1982	133,299
1983	142,892
1984	193,126
1985	141,619
1986	134,261
1987	139,189
1988	191,334
1989	160,639
1990	208,680
1991	189,435

Year	Total
1992	146,427
1993	141,000
1994	128,000
1995	180,000
1996	170,000
1997	176,000
1998	195,100
1999	157,000
2000	238,787
2001	178,000
2002	161,500
2003	183,000
2004	176,000
2005	223,000

Complete Scores

HOLE			1	2	3	4	5	6	7	8	9	10	11	12	13	14	15	16	17	18	
PAR	POSITION		4	4	4	4	5	4	4	3	4	4	3	4	4	5	4	4	4	4	TOTAL
Tiger Woods	1	Round 1	4	4	4	3	4	4	3	3	3	3	2	3	5	5	4	5	4	3	66
USA	1	Round 2	4	4	3	4	4	4	4	3	3	3	3	4	4	4	4	4	4	4	67
£720,000	1	Round 3	4	5	4	4	4	5	3	3	4	4	3	3	4	5	4	5	4	3	71
	1	Round 4	4	4	4	4	4	4	4	3	3	5	3	3	4	4	4	4	5	4	70 -**274**
Colin Montgomerie	T30	Round 1	5	4	4	4	4	4	3	4	4	3	4	4	4	4	4	4	4	4	71
Scotland	2	Round 2	3	4	3	4	3	4	4	4	3	3	3	5	5	4	3	4	4	3	66
£430,000	T3	Round 3	4	4	4	4	4	4	4	3	3	3	4	4	4	5	4	4	5	3	70
	2	Round 4	4	4	3	4	4	4	4	3	3	4	4	4	5	5	4	5	4	4	72 -**279**
Fred Couples	T3	Round 1	4	4	5	4	4	4	4	3	3	4	3	3	4	5	4	4	3	3	68
USA	T10	Round 2	4	4	4	4	5	4	4	3	4	4	3	4	5	3	5	4	4	3	71
£242,500	T22	Round 3	4	5	4	4	5	4	4	4	5	3	3	4	4	5	4	4	4	3	73
	T3	Round 4	3	4	4	4	5	4	4	3	3	3	3	4	4	5	4	4	4	3	68 -**280**
Jose M Olazabal	T3	Round 1	4	4	4	4	4	4	3	3	3	4	3	4	4	5	4	4	4	3	68
Spain	T3	Round 2	4	4	4	4	5	4	4	3	4	4	4	4	4	3	4	4	5	2	70
£242,500	2	Round 3	4	4	4	4	4	4	4	3	3	4	3	2	5	5	4	4	4	3	68
	T3	Round 4	4	4	4	3	5	5	4	3	3	4	3	5	5	5	5	4	5	3	74 -**280**
Geoff Ogilvy	T30	Round 1	3	4	4	4	5	4	4	3	3	4	3	4	5	5	5	4	4	3	71
Australia	T70	Round 2	4	4	5	5	3	4	4	3	3	4	4	4	4	5	5	4	4	5	74
£122,167	T22	Round 3	4	4	3	4	4	4	4	3	3	3	3	3	5	4	3	4	5	4	67
	T5	Round 4	4	5	4	5	5	5	3	3	3	4	3	3	4	5	3	4	3	3	69 -**281**
Bernhard Langer	T30	Round 1	4	3	4	4	5	3	4	3	4	4	4	5	5	5	3	3	5	3	71
Germany	T15	Round 2	4	4	4	5	4	3	4	3	3	3	2	4	5	5	5	4	4	3	69
£122,167	T9	Round 3	5	5	4	3	5	3	4	3	4	4	3	4	4	4	3	4	4	4	70
	T5	Round 4	4	4	4	4	3	4	4	3	3	5	3	4	4	4	6	4	5	3	71 -**281**
Vijay Singh	T13	Round 1	4	4	4	4	4	4	4	3	3	4	3	4	5	3	4	5	4	3	69
Fiji	T3	Round 2	3	4	4	4	5	4	4	3	3	4	3	4	4	4	4	4	4	4	69
£122,167	T7	Round 3	5	4	5	4	4	3	3	4	4	4	3	3	5	4	4	4	5	3	71
	T5	Round 4	3	4	4	4	5	4	5	2	4	4	3	3	5	5	5	4	5	3	72 -**281**
Michael Campbell	T13	Round 1	4	4	4	4	4	3	5	3	4	4	3	5	4	4	3	3	5	3	69
New Zealand	T25	Round 2	4	4	4	4	5	4	4	3	6	4	3	4	4	4	4	4	4	3	72
£122,167	T7	Round 3	4	3	5	4	5	5	3	2	3	4	3	4	4	4	4	4	4	3	68
	T5	Round 4	4	5	4	4	4	4	4	3	4	4	3	3	4	6	4	4	4	4	72 -**281**

* Denotes amateurs

	HOLE		1	2	3	4	5	6	7	8	9	10	11	12	13	14	15	16	17	18	
	PAR	POSITION	4	4	4	4	5	4	4	3	4	4	3	4	4	5	4	4	4	4	TOTAL
Sergio Garcia Spain £122,167	T21	Round 1	3	4	5	4	4	4	3	3	3	4	2	3	5	5	4	5	5	4	70
	T10	Round 2	4	4	3	5	4	4	4	3	5	3	3	3	4	5	4	4	4	3	69
	T5	Round 3	5	3	4	4	4	4	4	3	2	4	4	4	4	4	4	5	4	3	69
	T5	Round 4	4	5	4	4	4	4	4	3	4	4	3	6	5	4	3	4	5	3	73 **-281**
Retief Goosen South Africa £122,167	T3	Round 1	4	4	3	4	4	4	5	3	3	3	3	3	6	4	4	4	4	3	68
	T25	Round 2	4	4	4	4	5	4	4	4	4	4	4	3	4	4	5	4	5	3	73
	T3	Round 3	3	4	4	4	6	4	3	2	3	4	3	4	4	4	3	3	5	3	66
	T5	Round 4	5	5	4	4	6	4	4	4	3	4	3	5	4	4	4	4	4	3	74 **-281**
Graeme McDowell N. Ireland £66,750	T13	Round 1	4	4	4	4	4	4	4	4	4	2	4	5	4	4	4	4	4	3	69
	T25	Round 2	4	4	4	6	5	4	4	3	4	4	3	4	4	4	4	4	4	3	72
	T50	Round 3	3	4	4	4	4	4	4	3	4	4	3	4	5	4	4	4	8	4	74
	T11	Round 4	4	4	5	4	4	4	4	3	4	4	3	3	3	4	4	3	4	3	67 **-282**
Ian Poulter England £66,750	T21	Round 1	4	4	4	4	5	4	4	3	5	4	3	3	4	3	4	3	4	4	70
	T39	Round 2	4	5	4	5	6	4	4	3	5	4	3	4	4	5	3	3	3	3	72
	T29	Round 3	5	5	3	4	4	4	4	3	4	4	2	4	4	5	4	4	5	3	71
	T11	Round 4	4	4	3	4	5	3	4	3	3	4	3	4	4	4	4	4	5	4	69 **-282**
Nick Faldo England £66,750	T74	Round 1	4	4	4	5	4	4	4	3	4	4	4	4	4	6	4	4	5	3	74
	T47	Round 2	4	4	4	4	5	4	3	3	3	4	3	4	4	4	4	4	4	4	69
	T29	Round 3	4	4	3	4	4	4	4	3	4	4	3	4	5	5	4	4	4	3	70
	T11	Round 4	4	4	4	4	6	4	4	3	3	3	3	5	6	4	4	3	3	2	69 **-282**
Kenny Perry USA £66,750	T30	Round 1	4	4	3	4	5	4	3	3	3	4	3	5	6	5	3	4	5	3	71
	T39	Round 2	4	4	3	4	4	4	4	3	3	3	3	5	4	5	5	5	4	4	71
	T9	Round 3	4	4	3	3	4	4	4	3	4	3	3	4	4	6	3	4	4	4	68
	T11	Round 4	3	4	4	5	5	4	3	4	3	4	4	4	4	5	4	4	4	4	72 **-282**
David Frost South Africa £46,286	T128	Round 1	3	6	3	4	4	3	4	3	4	5	3	4	5	5	4	5	7	5	77
	T39	Round 2	4	3	4	4	4	3	3	3	4	3	3	4	5	3	4	4	4	3	65
	T39	Round 3	4	4	4	4	4	4	4	3	4	4	4	4	5	5	4	4	4	3	72
	T15	Round 4	3	4	4	4	4	4	4	3	4	4	3	3	5	4	4	4	4	4	69 **-283**
Nick O'Hern Australia £46,286	T56	Round 1	3	4	3	5	5	4	7	2	4	4	3	5	4	4	4	4	4	4	73
	T39	Round 2	3	4	3	4	5	4	4	3	3	4	2	4	4	4	5	4	5	4	69
	T29	Round 3	4	4	4	4	6	4	4	2	3	3	3	4	5	5	4	4	4	4	71
	T15	Round 4	4	4	4	4	4	5	4	3	4	4	3	4	3	5	4	4	4	3	70 **-283**
Mark Hensby Australia £46,286	2	Round 1	3	5	4	4	5	4	4	3	2	3	3	3	4	5	3	4	4	4	67
	T55	Round 2	5	7	3	7	5	4	4	3	4	4	3	4	4	5	4	4	4	3	77
	T29	Round 3	5	5	4	4	4	4	5	3	4	3	4	3	4	4	4	4	3	3	69
	T15	Round 4	6	3	4	4	5	4	4	3	3	4	3	3	4	4	4	3	5	4	70 **-283**
*Lloyd Saltman Scotland	T56	Round 1	4	4	4	4	4	4	3	4	4	4	3	3	5	4	4	5	6	4	73
	T55	Round 2	3	4	3	6	5	4	5	2	3	3	2	4	4	4	5	5	5	4	71
	T22	Round 3	4	4	4	4	4	4	4	3	3	4	2	4	3	6	4	3	4	4	68
	T15	Round 4	4	4	3	5	5	4	3	3	4	4	3	3	5	5	4	4	5	3	71 **-283**
Trevor Immelman South Africa £46,286	T3	Round 1	3	3	4	3	5	4	4	3	4	3	4	3	4	5	4	4	4	4	68
	T3	Round 2	4	5	3	5	5	4	4	3	3	4	3	3	5	4	4	4	4	3	70
	T20	Round 3	4	4	3	5	4	5	4	3	3	5	3	4	4	5	4	4	5	4	73
	T15	Round 4	4	5	4	4	4	5	4	3	3	5	3	4	4	4	4	5	4	3	72 **-283**
John Daly USA £46,286	T30	Round 1	4	4	4	5	5	4	3	2	3	4	3	4	5	6	3	4	4	4	71
	T15	Round 2	4	4	4	5	4	4	4	2	4	4	2	4	4	4	4	4	4	4	69
	T9	Round 3	3	3	3	4	5	4	4	3	4	5	3	3	5	6	4	4	4	3	70
	T15	Round 4	3	4	4	4	5	5	4	3	4	4	3	3	4	5	5	4	5	4	73 **-283**

HOLE			1	2	3	4	5	6	7	8	9	10	11	12	13	14	15	16	17	18	
PAR	POSITION		4	4	4	4	5	4	4	3	4	4	3	4	4	5	4	4	4	4	TOTAL
Sean O'Hair	T56	Round 1	4	5	4	4	4	4	3	3	3	4	3	5	5	5	4	4	5	4	73
USA	T15	Round 2	4	3	3	4	5	4	3	3	3	4	3	3	4	4	4	5	4	4	67
£46,286	T9	Round 3	4	4	4	4	5	4	4	3	3	5	3	3	4	4	4	4	4	4	70
	T15	Round 4	4	4	4	5	4	5	5	4	4	3	3	3	4	5	4	4	5	3	73 -**283**
Darren Clarke	T56	Round 1	4	4	3	5	5	4	3	4	4	4	4	4	4	4	3	5	5	4	73
N. Ireland	T47	Round 2	4	3	3	4	5	4	4	3	3	3	4	3	5	5	4	5	4	4	70
£46,286	T9	Round 3	3	5	4	4	4	3	3	2	4	5	4	3	3	5	4	3	4	4	67
	T15	Round 4	4	4	4	4	5	4	4	4	3	4	3	4	4	6	4	4	4	4	73 -**283**
*Eric Ramsay	T3	Round 1	4	5	4	5	5	3	3	3	3	3	4	4	4	4	3	4	4	3	68
Scotland	T39	Round 2	4	4	4	4	5	3	4	3	4	4	4	4	6	4	4	4	5	4	74
	T56	Round 3	5	4	4	4	5	4	4	3	5	4	3	4	5	5	4	4	4	3	74
	T23	Round 4	4	4	4	4	5	3	4	3	3	4	3	3	4	4	4	4	5	3	68 -**284**
Tom Lehman	T98	Round 1	4	4	4	4	4	6	4	4	5	4	3	5	4	5	4	4	4	3	75
USA	T55	Round 2	4	4	3	4	4	4	5	3	4	4	3	4	4	5	4	4	4	2	69
£32,500	T39	Round 3	3	4	3	5	4	4	4	3	4	4	3	3	4	5	4	5	4	4	70
	T23	Round 4	4	4	4	3	5	4	3	3	5	3	4	5	4	4	3	5	4	3	70 -**284**
Tadahiro Takayama	T41	Round 1	4	3	3	4	5	4	4	3	3	5	4	5	5	5	3	4	4	4	72
Japan	T55	Round 2	4	5	3	5	5	4	3	5	3	3	3	4	4	5	4	4	4	4	72
£32,500	T39	Round 3	5	3	3	3	4	4	3	4	3	4	3	5	4	5	4	5	5	3	70
	T23	Round 4	4	3	4	4	5	4	4	3	3	4	3	3	5	5	4	4	5	3	70 -**284**
Scott Drummond	T74	Round 1	5	3	4	5	4	4	5	4	4	4	3	4	4	4	4	5	5	4	74
Scotland	T70	Round 2	4	4	4	4	5	4	4	3	4	3	4	4	4	4	4	4	5	4	71
£32,500	T39	Round 3	4	4	3	3	4	4	4	3	3	4	3	4	4	4	4	5	5	5	69
	T23	Round 4	4	4	4	4	5	4	4	3	4	4	4	3	4	4	3	4	5	3	70 -**284**
Nick Flanagan	T56	Round 1	4	4	4	4	4	6	4	2	3	4	2	4	6	4	5	4	5	4	73
Australia	T55	Round 2	4	3	4	4	4	4	4	4	4	3	4	5	5	5	5	4	4	3	71
£32,500	T29	Round 3	4	4	3	4	4	3	4	3	4	4	3	4	5	5	4	4	4	3	69
	T23	Round 4	5	4	3	4	4	4	4	4	3	4	3	4	4	5	4	4	4	4	71 -**284**
Scott Verplank	T3	Round 1	3	6	3	4	4	4	4	3	3	4	3	4	5	4	4	4	3	3	68
USA	T3	Round 2	4	4	3	7	3	4	4	2	4	3	3	4	4	4	4	5	5	3	70
£32,500	T9	Round 3	3	4	4	5	4	4	4	3	5	4	3	3	5	5	5	4	4	3	72
	T23	Round 4	4	4	4	4	4	4	4	4	3	5	3	4	6	4	4	5	4	4	74 -**284**
Bart Bryant	T13	Round 1	4	4	5	3	3	4	5	3	3	4	3	4	4	6	3	4	4	3	69
USA	T10	Round 2	4	4	4	4	5	4	4	3	3	4	3	4	4	5	4	4	4	3	70
£32,500	T9	Round 3	4	4	4	3	5	4	5	3	3	5	3	3	4	5	5	4	4	3	71
	T23	Round 4	4	4	4	4	5	4	4	3	5	3	3	4	6	4	4	5	4	4	74 -**284**
Tim Clark	T30	Round 1	3	5	4	4	4	4	5	3	3	3	3	4	4	5	4	5	5	3	71
South Africa	T15	Round 2	4	4	3	4	4	4	4	3	4	3	3	4	3	6	4	4	4	4	69
£32,500	T9	Round 3	3	3	3	4	4	4	4	3	5	4	3	3	5	5	4	5	4	4	70
	T23	Round 4	4	5	4	4	4	5	5	4	3	4	4	4	4	5	4	3	5	3	74 -**284**
Brad Faxon	T41	Round 1	3	4	4	4	6	3	4	3	4	4	3	5	4	4	4	4	5	4	72
USA	T3	Round 2	4	3	3	4	4	4	4	2	3	4	3	4	4	5	4	4	4	3	66
£32,500	T5	Round 3	4	4	4	6	4	3	4	4	3	4	3	4	4	4	5	3	4	3	70
	T23	Round 4	6	4	4	4	5	4	4	3	3	5	2	6	4	6	4	4	4	4	76 -**284**
Richard Green	T41	Round 1	4	4	4	3	4	3	4	3	4	4	4	4	4	6	4	4	5	4	72
Australia	T15	Round 2	4	4	4	4	4	4	4	3	3	4	3	3	4	4	4	4	5	3	68
£26,500	T22	Round 3	4	4	3	4	5	4	4	4	3	4	4	4	5	5	3	5	5	3	72
	T32	Round 4	4	5	4	4	5	4	5	3	3	4	3	4	4	6	5	3	4	3	73 -**285**

HOLE			1	2	3	4	5	6	7	8	9	10	11	12	13	14	15	16	17	18	
PAR	POSITION		4	4	4	4	5	4	4	3	4	4	3	4	4	5	4	4	4	4	TOTAL
Sandy Lyle	T74	Round 1	4	4	4	4	4	4	4	4	4	4	3	4	4	5	4	4	7	3	74
Scotland	T25	Round 2	3	4	3	4	4	5	4	2	3	4	3	3	4	5	4	4	4	4	67
£26,500	T9	Round 3	4	4	4	4	5	4	4	3	3	4	3	3	5	4	5	3	4	3	69
	T32	Round 4	5	4	4	4	4	5	3	3	5	5	3	4	5	5	5	4	4	3	75 -285
Joe Ogilvie	T74	Round 1	4	3	4	4	5	4	5	4	4	4	4	5	4	6	4	4	3	3	74
USA	T55	Round 2	4	5	4	4	4	4	4	3	3	4	3	4	4	5	4	3	4	4	70
£22,000	T66	Round 3	3	4	3	4	4	4	4	3	3	4	4	5	5	6	5	4	5	3	73
	T34	Round 4	4	5	4	4	4	3	4	3	3	3	3	4	4	5	4	4	4	4	69 -286
Ernie Els	T74	Round 1	4	4	3	3	6	4	4	3	4	4	4	5	5	5	4	4	4	4	74
South Africa	T25	Round 2	3	3	4	5	4	3	3	3	4	3	4	4	5	4	4	4	4	3	67
£22,000	T56	Round 3	5	4	4	5	5	4	3	3	3	5	4	4	4	5	4	4	5	4	75
	T34	Round 4	3	5	4	4	4	4	3	2	3	3	3	4	4	7	4	5	4	4	70 -286
Thomas Levet	T13	Round 1	4	3	4	4	4	4	5	3	5	3	3	4	4	3	3	4	5	4	69
France	T15	Round 2	3	4	4	4	3	4	4	4	3	4	3	4	4	6	4	5	4	4	71
£22,000	T50	Round 3	4	4	5	6	6	4	3	3	4	3	4	4	5	5	4	4	4	4	75
	T34	Round 4	4	4	4	5	4	4	3	3	4	4	3	4	5	4	4	5	4	3	71 -286
Peter Hanson	T41	Round 1	4	4	4	4	6	5	4	3	4	4	3	5	4	4	3	4	4	3	72
Sweden	T55	Round 2	4	4	4	4	4	4	4	3	4	4	4	3	4	4	5	5	6	3	72
£22,000	T50	Round 3	3	4	4	3	5	4	3	3	3	4	3	4	4	6	5	4	4	5	71
	T34	Round 4	4	4	3	4	4	5	3	3	4	4	4	3	5	4	5	4	4	4	71 -286
Henrik Stenson	T74	Round 1	4	3	4	4	6	5	4	3	4	5	3	4	5	5	4	4	5	2	74
Sweden	T25	Round 2	4	3	4	5	4	4	3	3	4	4	2	4	4	4	3	5	4	3	67
£22,000	T39	Round 3	4	6	4	4	4	4	3	3	4	4	2	5	5	4	4	5	5	3	73
	T34	Round 4	3	4	4	4	5	5	4	4	4	4	3	4	5	4	3	4	5	3	72 -286
Simon Dyson	T21	Round 1	4	5	4	4	4	4	4	4	2	4	3	4	3	5	5	4	4	3	70
England	T25	Round 2	4	3	4	4	4	4	4	3	3	3	3	4	4	6	5	5	4	4	71
£22,000	T29	Round 3	4	3	4	4	5	4	4	3	4	5	4	4	4	5	4	4	4	3	72
	T34	Round 4	3	5	4	5	4	4	3	3	4	4	3	5	5	4	4	4	5	4	73 -286
Adam Scott	T21	Round 1	3	4	4	4	4	5	4	3	4	4	3	4	4	4	3	4	5	4	70
Australia	T25	Round 2	4	4	4	4	5	3	4	3	5	4	2	3	4	5	4	5	4	4	71
£22,000	T20	Round 3	4	4	4	3	5	4	4	3	3	4	3	4	5	4	4	4	5	3	70
	T34	Round 4	4	5	4	5	4	6	4	3	3	4	3	3	4	5	4	4	5	5	75 -286
Paul McGinley	T21	Round 1	3	4	4	5	5	4	4	3	3	4	3	4	4	5	3	5	3	4	70
Ireland	T70	Round 2	4	4	5	5	5	4	3	3	4	4	3	4	4	6	4	3	6	4	75
£14,977	T70	Round 3	4	4	4	4	5	4	4	2	6	3	3	3	4	5	5	4	6	3	73
	T41	Round 4	3	3	4	5	4	4	4	3	3	3	3	4	4	4	4	4	6	4	69 -287
Simon Khan	T13	Round 1	4	4	4	5	4	4	4	3	4	3	4	4	3	4	4	4	4	3	69
England	T10	Round 2	4	4	4	4	4	4	4	3	3	4	4	3	5	4	4	4	4	4	70
£14,977	T66	Round 3	4	5	4	3	6	5	4	2	5	4	6	3	6	5	4	4	4	4	78
	T41	Round 4	4	4	3	4	4	3	3	2	4	4	4	5	4	5	4	4	5	4	70 -287
Tom Watson	T98	Round 1	3	5	4	5	4	4	3	4	4	4	3	5	5	5	4	4	5	4	75
USA	T70	Round 2	4	5	4	5	5	4	3	3	3	4	3	4	4	4	3	4	4	4	70
£14,977	T50	Round 3	4	4	3	4	4	4	5	3	3	4	4	6	4	4	3	3	5	3	70
	T41	Round 4	6	4	4	4	4	3	4	3	4	4	3	5	4	4	4	4	5	3	72 -287
Hiroyuki Fujita	T41	Round 1	4	5	3	5	4	4	4	3	3	5	2	5	5	4	4	4	5	3	72
Japan	T15	Round 2	3	4	4	5	4	4	3	3	4	3	3	4	5	5	4	4	3	3	68
£14,977	T39	Round 3	4	4	4	5	5	3	5	3	4	4	3	4	5	4	4	5	4	4	74
	T41	Round 4	4	4	4	5	4	4	4	3	3	4	3	5	5	4	4	5	5	3	73 -287

HOLE			1	2	3	4	5	6	7	8	9	10	11	12	13	14	15	16	17	18	
PAR	POSITION		4	4	4	4	5	4	4	3	4	4	3	4	4	5	4	4	4	4	TOTAL
Steve Webster	T30	Round 1	3	4	4	4	3	4	4	2	2	5	4	4	6	5	4	5	4	4	71
England	T47	Round 2	4	4	4	4	4	4	4	4	4	3	3	4	4	5	4	4	5	4	72
£14,977	T39	Round 3	4	4	4	4	4	4	4	3	3	3	2	4	4	7	4	4	4	5	71
	T41	Round 4	4	5	3	4	5	4	4	3	4	4	3	4	5	5	4	4	5	3	73 **-287**
K J Choi	T98	Round 1	4	4	4	4	5	5	5	3	3	4	4	3	5	5	4	4	4	5	75
Korea	T47	Round 2	4	4	4	4	4	4	4	2	4	3	3	4	4	4	5	4	4	3	68
£14,977	T39	Round 3	4	4	4	4	5	3	4	3	5	4	3	4	4	4	4	4	5	3	71
	T41	Round 4	3	4	4	4	4	4	4	3	4	3	4	3	4	4	4	4	9	4	73 **-287**
Tim Herron	T56	Round 1	3	4	4	4	5	5	4	3	4	4	3	4	6	5	3	4	5	3	73
USA	T70	Round 2	4	4	4	5	5	3	4	3	4	3	3	4	5	6	4	4	4	3	72
£14,977	T29	Round 3	4	4	4	4	4	4	3	3	3	3	3	3	4	4	4	6	5	3	68
	T41	Round 4	3	4	5	4	5	5	3	3	4	5	3	3	5	5	4	4	5	4	74 **-287**
Stuart Appleby	T41	Round 1	3	6	3	4	5	3	4	3	3	4	3	5	4	5	4	4	5	4	72
Australia	T15	Round 2	3	3	4	5	4	4	3	3	3	3	3	4	4	4	4	5	5	4	68
£14,977	T22	Round 3	4	4	4	4	5	4	3	2	4	4	3	4	4	6	5	4	5	4	72
	T41	Round 4	5	4	4	4	5	4	4	3	3	5	3	4	5	5	4	4	4	4	75 **-287**
Bob Tway	T13	Round 1	5	4	4	4	4	4	5	3	4	3	2	3	4	5	4	4	4	3	69
USA	T15	Round 2	3	4	4	4	5	4	4	3	4	4	3	4	3	5	5	3	5	4	71
£14,977	T22	Round 3	4	4	4	4	5	4	4	3	4	4	3	4	5	4	4	4	4	4	72
	T41	Round 4	4	5	4	4	6	4	4	3	4	4	3	4	5	5	4	4	5	3	75 **-287**
Maarten Lafeber	T56	Round 1	3	4	4	5	5	5	4	3	4	5	3	4	4	4	4	4	4	3	73
Netherlands	T47	Round 2	4	5	4	4	5	3	4	3	3	4	4	4	4	4	4	4	4	4	70
£14,977	T9	Round 3	4	4	3	4	4	4	3	2	3	4	3	4	4	4	5	4	4	4	67
	T41	Round 4	4	5	5	5	5	4	4	3	4	4	3	5	4	6	4	5	3	4	77 **-287**
Soren Hansen	T41	Round 1	4	4	4	4	4	4	4	3	4	4	3	5	3	6	4	4	5	3	72
Denmark	T55	Round 2	4	4	4	4	4	4	4	4	3	4	4	4	5	4	4	4	5	3	72
£14,977	T9	Round 3	4	4	3	4	4	4	4	2	3	3	3	3	4	7	4	4	4	2	66
	T41	Round 4	4	7	4	5	5	3	5	3	3	3	3	3	5	6	5	4	6	3	77 **-287**
Justin Leonard	T56	Round 1	4	5	4	5	5	5	4	3	4	3	4	3	4	4	4	4	4	4	73
USA	T55	Round 2	5	5	4	5	3	4	4	3	4	3	3	4	4	5	4	4	4	3	71
£10,931	T73	Round 3	4	4	4	4	5	4	4	3	6	4	3	3	5	7	4	3	5	3	75
	T52	Round 4	4	4	4	4	5	5	3	3	3	4	3	3	4	4	4	4	4	4	69 **-288**
Luke Donald	T3	Round 1	4	4	3	4	4	4	4	3	3	4	4	4	3	4	4	4	4	4	68
England	T25	Round 2	4	6	3	5	4	3	4	3	4	3	3	5	4	5	4	4	5	4	73
£10,931	T70	Round 3	3	4	5	4	5	5	5	3	2	4	4	4	4	5	5	5	6	4	77
	T52	Round 4	4	4	4	5	5	3	2	3	3	4	3	4	3	5	4	5	6	3	70 **-288**
Paul Lawrie	T41	Round 1	3	4	4	4	6	5	3	4	3	4	3	3	4	5	4	4	6	3	72
Scotland	T47	Round 2	4	4	4	4	4	4	4	3	3	4	3	4	4	5	5	4	5	3	71
£10,931	T70	Round 3	4	4	4	4	5	4	4	3	4	3	4	4	4	6	4	4	6	4	75
	T52	Round 4	4	5	4	5	4	4	3	3	4	3	3	3	4	5	4	4	4	3	70 **-288**
Robert Allenby	T21	Round 1	3	4	3	4	4	4	4	4	3	4	3	6	4	4	4	4	6	3	70
Australia	T3	Round 2	4	4	3	4	5	4	3	3	3	4	2	3	4	6	4	4	4	4	68
£10,931	T66	Round 3	4	4	4	4	6	4	7	3	4	4	3	6	5	4	5	5	4	4	79
	T52	Round 4	4	5	4	5	4	5	3	4	3	5	3	4	4	4	4	3	4	3	71 **-288**
Miguel A Jimenez	T13	Round 1	4	3	5	4	4	4	3	4	3	4	3	4	5	4	4	4	4	3	69
Spain	T25	Round 2	3	5	4	5	6	4	5	3	3	4	3	4	4	4	4	4	4	3	72
£10,931	T66	Round 3	3	4	3	4	5	4	4	3	4	5	3	4	5	5	4	5	6	5	76
	T52	Round 4	5	5	3	4	4	4	3	3	3	5	3	4	5	4	5	4	4	3	71 **-288**

HOLE			1	2	3	4	5	6	7	8	9	10	11	12	13	14	15	16	17	18	
PAR	POSITION		4	4	4	4	5	4	4	3	4	4	3	4	4	5	4	4	4	4	TOTAL
Thongchai Jaidee	T56	Round 1	5	4	5	4	4	4	3	3	5	4	3	5	4	5	4	5	3	3	73
Thailand	T25	Round 2	4	5	4	4	4	3	4	3	4	4	3	3	4	4	4	5	3	68
£10,931	T56	Round 3	4	5	5	4	4	4	5	3	4	4	3	4	5	5	4	5	5	2	75
	T52	Round 4	5	4	4	3	5	4	4	3	4	3	3	4	4	5	4	4	6	3	72 **-288**
Fredrik Jacobson	T30	Round 1	4	4	3	5	4	4	4	3	3	4	3	4	5	4	4	6	4	3	71
Sweden	T25	Round 2	3	5	4	3	6	4	3	3	4	6	3	3	4	5	4	4	4	2	70
£10,931	T29	Round 3	4	4	4	5	4	3	4	2	3	4	4	4	5	6	5	3	4	4	72
	T52	Round 4	4	4	3	4	5	4	4	3	3	5	3	5	4	5	5	4	7	3	75 **-288**
Bo Van Pelt	T41	Round 1	4	4	4	4	5	5	4	3	4	5	3	4	4	4	4	4	4	3	72
USA	T10	Round 2	4	4	4	4	4	4	4	2	3	3	3	5	4	4	3	4	4	4	67
£10,931	T22	Round 3	4	4	3	5	6	5	4	3	4	4	3	3	4	5	4	4	3	4	73
	T52	Round 4	4	3	6	5	4	5	5	3	5	4	3	5	3	4	5	5	5	2	76 **-288**
Tino Schuster	T3	Round 1	4	4	3	4	4	4	3	4	3	4	3	4	4	4	4	4	4	4	68
Germany	T39	Round 2	4	4	4	4	4	3	4	2	4	4	5	5	6	4	4	6	4	74
£10,000	T56	Round 3	4	4	6	4	5	3	4	3	4	4	3	4	4	4	4	5	5	4	74
	T60	Round 4	4	4	4	5	4	4	3	4	4	3	4	6	4	5	3	4	5	4	73 **-289**
Mark Calcavecchia	T21	Round 1	3	5	4	4	4	4	5	3	3	5	3	3	5	4	4	4	4	3	70
USA	T47	Round 2	3	4	4	5	4	4	4	2	4	3	4	4	4	5	5	5	5	4	73
£10,000	T56	Round 3	4	5	4	4	5	5	5	3	3	4	3	3	4	4	4	5	4	73
	T60	Round 4	4	4	3	4	4	5	4	3	4	4	3	4	3	5	5	5	5	4	73 **-289**
John Bickerton	T98	Round 1	4	4	4	4	5	4	4	3	4	4	3	4	5	6	4	4	5	4	75
England	T70	Round 2	3	3	4	4	5	4	4	3	4	3	4	3	4	7	4	4	4	4	70
£10,000	T56	Round 3	4	4	5	4	4	3	3	3	4	4	4	4	6	4	4	4	3	71
	T60	Round 4	3	4	4	4	5	5	4	3	4	4	3	3	4	4	6	4	4	5	73 **-289**
***Edoardo Molinari**	T21	Round 1	4	4	5	4	5	4	3	3	3	4	3	5	4	4	4	4	4	4	70
Italy	T15	Round 2	3	5	4	4	5	4	4	2	4	4	3	4	3	4	5	4	4	4	70
	T39	Round 3	4	4	4	4	5	4	4	3	3	4	3	4	5	5	4	5	5	4	74
	T60	Round 4	5	4	4	5	4	4	4	3	4	4	3	4	4	5	5	4	5	4	75 **-289**
Phil Mickelson	T74	Round 1	4	4	3	4	5	4	4	3	4	4	3	5	4	5	7	4	5	3	74
USA	T25	Round 2	5	3	4	4	4	4	5	2	3	4	2	3	4	4	4	4	5	3	67
£10,000	T29	Round 3	4	4	4	4	5	3	3	3	3	3	3	5	6	5	4	4	5	4	72
	T60	Round 4	4	5	4	5	5	5	4	3	4	4	4	5	4	4	5	4	4	3	76 **-289**
Greg Norman	T41	Round 1	4	4	5	5	3	4	5	4	3	4	4	4	4	4	4	4	4	3	72
Australia	T47	Round 2	4	3	4	5	5	4	4	4	3	3	3	4	4	6	4	4	4	3	71
£10,000	T29	Round 3	4	4	4	4	6	4	3	3	3	4	3	4	4	5	4	4	4	3	70
	T60	Round 4	4	4	3	4	5	4	6	3	4	4	4	5	4	5	4	4	4	5	76 **-289**
Peter Lonard	T3	Round 1	4	3	3	6	5	4	3	3	3	3	3	5	6	3	3	4	4	3	68
Australia	T3	Round 2	4	4	3	4	5	3	5	3	3	4	5	4	4	5	3	3	5	3	70
£9,700	T50	Round 3	4	3	4	4	6	6	5	3	5	4	3	4	5	5	4	4	5	3	77
	66	Round 4	5	5	3	4	4	4	4	3	5	4	3	4	5	5	4	6	4	3	75 **-290**
Duffy Waldorf	T74	Round 1	6	4	4	4	4	4	4	2	4	4	2	5	4	4	4	4	7	4	74
USA	T39	Round 2	3	4	4	4	4	4	3	4	4	4	4	3	4	4	3	4	4	4	68
£9,350	79	Round 3	4	4	4	4	6	6	4	3	4	4	4	5	5	7	5	5	4	3	81
	T67	Round 4	4	4	4	4	4	4	4	3	3	3	3	4	4	5	4	4	4	3	68 **-291**
Robert Rock	T56	Round 1	4	5	4	4	6	4	4	4	3	3	3	5	4	5	5	3	4	3	73
England	T55	Round 2	4	5	4	5	4	4	4	4	3	4	2	3	5	4	4	4	4	4	71
£9,350	T73	Round 3	4	4	4	6	5	4	4	3	3	5	3	4	5	5	5	3	4	4	75
	T67	Round 4	3	5	4	4	4	4	4	3	3	4	3	4	4	6	4	5	5	3	72 **-291**

HOLE			1	2	3	4	5	6	7	8	9	10	11	12	13	14	15	16	17	18	
PAR	POSITION		4	4	4	4	5	4	4	3	4	4	3	4	4	5	4	4	4	4	TOTAL
Chris Riley	T3	Round 1	3	4	4	5	4	4	4	3	3	4	3	4	4	4	4	4	3	4	68
USA	T25	Round 2	5	4	4	5	4	4	4	3	4	4	2	4	5	4	4	4	5	4	73
£9,350	T56	Round 3	4	4	4	5	4	4	5	4	6	3	3	4	4	5	4	4	4	4	75
	T67	Round 4	4	4	4	4	5	4	4	3	5	4	3	4	4	5	4	4	7	3	75 **-291**
Chris DiMarco	T98	Round 1	4	4	4	5	4	5	4	3	4	5	4	3	4	5	4	4	5	4	75
USA	T55	Round 2	3	3	4	5	6	4	4	3	3	4	3	2	4	5	4	4	4	4	69
£9,350	T50	Round 3	4	4	4	4	4	4	4	3	5	4	3	3	5	5	4	3	5	3	71
	T67	Round 4	6	4	4	4	4	4	4	4	5	4	3	5	4	5	4	4	5	3	76 **-291**
Pat Perez	T41	Round 1	4	4	5	5	4	4	5	3	4	4	3	4	4	4	4	4	4	3	72
USA	T39	Round 2	4	4	4	5	5	4	4	3	2	4	3	3	4	5	5	4	5	3	70
£9,350	T39	Round 3	4	5	4	4	4	4	4	4	3	4	4	3	4	5	4	4	5	3	72
	T67	Round 4	4	5	4	4	4	4	6	4	4	4	3	4	5	5	4	4	5	4	77 **-291**
David Smail	T56	Round 1	3	4	4	5	5	4	4	3	3	4	3	5	4	6	4	4	4	4	73
New Zealand	T70	Round 2	4	4	4	4	4	5	4	3	4	4	3	3	5	6	4	4	4	3	72
£9,350	T39	Round 3	4	5	3	4	4	3	3	3	4	5	3	4	4	5	4	4	4	3	69
	T67	Round 4	5	4	4	4	5	4	5	3	4	3	5	5	5	4	4	4	5	4	77 **-291**
Patrik Sjoland	T74	Round 1	3	4	4	4	6	4	4	4	5	3	2	4	5	5	4	4	4	5	74
Sweden	T70	Round 2	3	4	3	4	5	3	4	3	5	4	3	4	5	6	4	4	4	3	71
£9,000	T76	Round 3	4	7	4	4	5	4	3	3	4	4	3	5	5	5	5	4	4	3	76
	73	Round 4	4	4	3	4	5	4	4	3	4	4	3	4	4	5	4	4	3	5	71 **-292**
Ted Purdy	T41	Round 1	4	3	3	4	5	4	4	4	3	4	3	4	5	6	4	4	4	4	72
USA	T55	Round 2	6	4	4	4	4	3	4	4	3	4	3	4	4	5	3	4	5	4	72
£8,800	T76	Round 3	4	4	5	4	5	4	4	4	4	6	4	4	4	5	4	5	4	4	77
	T74	Round 4	4	3	4	3	4	4	4	4	3	4	3	4	5	5	6	4	4	4	72 **-293**
Scott Gutschewski	T116	Round 1	4	4	4	4	8	4	5	3	3	4	4	4	5	6	4	3	3	4	76
USA	T70	Round 2	4	4	3	3	4	4	4	3	4	3	4	4	4	5	5	4	4	3	69
£8,800	75	Round 3	4	4	4	6	4	5	4	3	3	4	3	3	5	4	4	4	8	3	75
	T74	Round 4	6	4	3	4	3	4	3	3	3	3	3	5	5	4	4	7	5	4	73 **-293**
S K Ho	T56	Round 1	3	4	5	5	3	4	4	3	4	4	3	5	4	6	4	5	4	4	73
Korea	T55	Round 2	4	5	4	4	5	4	4	4	4	3	3	3	5	4	4	4	4	3	71
£8,800	T56	Round 3	3	5	4	4	5	4	4	2	4	4	3	6	4	4	5	4	4	3	72
	T74	Round 4	4	4	5	4	5	4	4	3	5	4	3	5	5	5	4	5	4	4	77 **-293**
Steve Flesch	T74	Round 1	4	4	3	5	4	4	3	4	4	4	3	4	5	6	5	4	5	3	74
USA	T55	Round 2	3	3	4	4	5	3	3	3	4	4	3	4	4	5	4	4	6	4	70
£8,600	T56	Round 3	3	4	4	4	5	4	4	3	3	4	3	3	4	6	5	4	5	4	72
	77	Round 4	4	4	3	4	6	4	4	4	3	4	4	5	4	5	6	5	6	3	78 **-294**
Graeme Storm	T98	Round 1	6	4	4	4	5	5	4	3	4	4	2	5	4	6	4	4	4	3	75
England	T70	Round 2	4	4	4	4	4	4	4	3	3	3	6	4	4	4	4	4	4	3	70
£8,450	80	Round 3	4	4	4	5	6	4	4	3	3	4	4	5	5	5	4	5	8	3	80
	T78	Round 4	4	6	3	5	4	4	4	3	3	3	3	4	4	4	4	4	5	4	71 **-296**
Rod Pampling	T74	Round 1	4	4	4	4	5	4	4	3	4	4	3	4	4	5	4	7	4	3	74
Australia	T70	Round 2	4	4	4	4	4	3	7	3	3	4	3	3	4	5	4	4	4	4	71
£8,450	T56	Round 3	3	4	4	4	4	3	4	2	5	4	3	5	4	4	4	6	5	3	71
	T78	Round 4	4	4	4	5	5	4	4	4	4	4	3	4	5	8	5	6	4	3	80 **-296**
*Matthew Richardson	T98	Round 1	5	4	4	4	5	4	4	3	4	3	3	4	5	6	4	5	5	3	75
England	T55	Round 2	3	4	4	4	4	4	4	3	4	4	4	3	4	5	4	4	4	3	69
	T76	Round 3	5	4	4	4	5	4	4	3	6	4	3	4	4	5	5	4	5	4	77
	80	Round 4	4	5	4	4	5	4	4	3	5	4	3	5	5	5	4	4	5	3	76 **-297**

NON QUALIFIERS AFTER 36 HOLES

(Leading 10 professionals and ties receive £3,000 each, next 20 professionals and ties receive £2,500 each, next 20 professionals and ties receive £2,250 each, remainder of professionals receive £2,000 each.)

HOLE			1	2	3	4	5	6	7	8	9	10	11	12	13	14	15	16	17	18	
PAR	POSITION		4	4	4	4	5	4	4	3	4	4	3	4	5	4	4	4	4	4	TOTAL
Alex Cejka	T74	Round 1	4	4	3	5	5	4	5	3	5	4	3	4	5	4	4	4	5	3	74
Germany	**T81**	Round 2	4	5	4	3	4	4	4	3	4	4	2	5	4	5	4	4	4	5	72 -146
Peter Fowler	T74	Round 1	5	5	4	5	5	4	3	3	4	4	4	4	4	4	4	4	4	4	74
Australia	**T81**	Round 2	4	4	4	4	5	3	3	4	4	4	3	5	4	4	4	4	5	4	72 -146
Daniel Chopra	T116	Round 1	6	4	4	4	5	5	3	3	4	5	3	5	5	4	5	4	4	3	76
Sweden	**T81**	Round 2	4	3	4	4	4	3	4	3	3	5	4	4	4	5	4	4	4	4	70 -146
Joe Durant	T146	Round 1	4	5	5	5	6	4	6	3	4	6	3	4	4	5	4	4	4	3	79
USA	**T81**	Round 2	4	4	3	5	3	4	4	3	3	4	3	4	4	4	3	4	5	3	67 -146
Peter Baker	T21	Round 1	4	4	4	5	4	4	4	3	4	4	4	4	4	4	4	4	4	3	70
England	**T81**	Round 2	4	3	4	5	3	5	5	3	4	4	3	4	5	5	4	6	5	4	76 -146
Lee Westwood	T116	Round 1	6	4	4	4	5	4	4	3	4	4	4	4	5	5	3	5	5	4	76
England	**T81**	Round 2	3	4	3	5	4	4	4	3	4	3	3	4	4	5	4	4	7	3	70 -146
Charles Howell III	T30	Round 1	4	4	3	4	5	4	4	3	5	3	4	4	5	4	4	4	4	4	71
USA	**T81**	Round 2	4	5	3	5	4	4	4	3	4	4	4	3	5	5	5	4	5	4	75 -146
Stephen Dodd	T98	Round 1	3	4	4	4	4	4	5	4	4	4	3	5	4	5	4	5	6	3	75
Wales	**T81**	Round 2	4	4	4	5	4	5	4	3	3	3	3	3	5	5	3	5	5	4	71 -146
Mark O'Meara	T30	Round 1	5	4	3	4	4	4	3	2	4	3	4	4	4	6	4	5	4	4	71
USA	**T81**	Round 2	4	5	4	5	4	4	4	3	5	4	3	5	5	4	5	4	4	3	75 -146
Thomas Bjorn	T41	Round 1	4	5	3	4	5	3	5	3	5	4	3	4	4	6	3	4	4	3	72
Denmark	**T81**	Round 2	4	5	4	4	5	4	3	4	3	4	2	4	5	4	4	4	5	6	74 -146
Euan Walters	T41	Round 1	4	5	4	5	4	4	4	3	4	4	3	4	5	5	4	4	4	3	72
Australia	**T81**	Round 2	4	5	4	5	4	3	4	4	3	4	3	4	4	6	5	3	4	5	74 -146
Mardan Mamat	T98	Round 1	4	4	4	4	4	4	5	3	5	3	3	4	5	4	5	4	6	4	75
Singapore	**T92**	Round 2	4	4	4	5	4	5	4	3	3	4	3	3	4	5	4	5	5	4	72 -147
Jerry Kelly	T74	Round 1	4	4	4	4	7	4	4	3	4	4	2	3	4	5	5	4	5	4	74
USA	**T92**	Round 2	5	4	3	5	6	4	4	3	3	4	3	4	4	4	4	4	6	3	73 -147
Jack Nicklaus	T98	Round 1	3	5	4	5	5	4	3	3	4	4	4	5	5	5	4	4	4	4	75
USA	**T92**	Round 2	4	5	4	4	4	4	4	3	4	3	3	5	4	5	4	4	5	3	72 -147
Alastair Forsyth	T128	Round 1	4	6	4	4	4	5	5	4	3	4	3	4	4	7	4	4	4	4	77
Scotland	**T92**	Round 2	4	4	4	4	4	3	4	3	4	3	3	4	4	5	4	4	5	4	70 -147
Zach Johnson	T128	Round 1	4	4	4	5	5	4	4	3	4	3	3	4	4	5	4	4	9	4	77
USA	**T92**	Round 2	3	4	3	4	4	4	4	3	4	4	4	4	5	4	4	5	4	3	70 -147
Jean F Remesy	T56	Round 1	3	5	3	6	4	4	4	3	3	3	4	4	5	6	4	4	5	3	73
France	**T92**	Round 2	4	4	4	4	5	4	4	4	4	4	4	4	5	5	4	4	4	3	74 -147
Danny Chia	T74	Round 1	5	6	3	4	3	4	4	4	4	3	2	4	5	7	5	3	6	2	74
Malasia	**T92**	Round 2	4	4	5	4	4	4	3	4	3	4	3	4	4	5	5	4	5	4	73 -147
Yong-Eun Yang	T116	Round 1	4	5	4	4	5	5	4	3	5	4	4	4	4	5	4	5	4	3	76
Korea	**T92**	Round 2	4	4	3	4	4	4	3	5	4	3	4	4	4	5	4	4	5	3	71 -147
Tom Byrum	T146	Round 1	4	5	5	4	4	5	4	5	4	5	3	4	4	6	4	4	5	4	79
USA	**T100**	Round 2	4	4	4	4	5	4	3	3	2	4	3	3	4	5	4	4	5	4	69 -148
Fred Funk	T128	Round 1	4	3	4	6	5	5	4	4	4	4	3	4	4	5	4	6	4	4	77
USA	**T100**	Round 2	4	4	4	4	5	4	4	3	4	4	2	4	4	4	4	4	5	4	71 -148

	POSITION		1	2	3	4	5	6	7	8	9	10	11	12	13	14	15	16	17	18	TOTAL
PAR			4	4	4	4	5	4	4	3	4	4	3	4	4	5	4	4	4	4	
Nick Price	T116	Round 1	4	4	3	5	5	4	4	3	5	5	4	3	5	6	4	4	5	3	76
Zimbabwe	**T100**	Round 2	4	4	4	5	5	4	4	3	3	4	5	4	4	5	3	4	4	3	72 -**148**
Jim Furyk	T138	Round 1	4	4	4	4	7	4	6	4	5	4	4	4	4	5	3	5	4	3	78
USA	**T100**	Round 2	4	3	5	5	6	4	4	3	5	4	2	4	3	4	4	4	3	3	70 -**148**
Ben Curtis	T138	Round 1	4	4	4	5	5	4	4	3	3	5	4	5	5	6	5	4	5	3	78
USA	**T100**	Round 2	4	3	4	4	6	4	3	2	4	4	3	3	5	5	4	4	5	3	70 -**148**
Ian Woosnam	T56	Round 1	5	4	4	4	5	4	4	3	3	4	2	4	5	5	4	4	6	3	73
Wales	**T100**	Round 2	4	4	3	4	5	4	4	3	4	3	6	5	4	5	4	5	5	3	75 -**148**
Joakim Haeggman	T98	Round 1	4	5	3	4	4	5	4	3	4	4	4	4	5	5	4	4	5	4	75
Sweden	**T100**	Round 2	5	3	4	4	4	5	4	2	4	4	4	3	4	4	5	6	4		73 -**148**
Jason Allred	T74	Round 1	3	5	5	3	6	4	4	4	4	4	3	5	4	5	4	4	4	3	74
USA	**T100**	Round 2	4	3	4	4	4	4	4	3	4	4	4	4	5	4	5	5	5	4	74 -**148**
Todd Hamilton	T74	Round 1	4	5	4	4	5	6	4	3	4	4	3	4	5	5	3	3	5	3	74
USA	**T100**	Round 2	3	5	4	4	5	4	5	3	3	4	3	4	6	5	5	4	3	4	74 -**148**
Shaun Micheel	T98	Round 1	4	4	4	4	4	4	4	4	4	3	5	6	5	3	5	4	3		75
USA	**T100**	Round 2	4	4	4	4	5	4	4	2	5	4	2	4	4	4	4	5	7	3	73 -**148**
Andrew Oldcorn	T116	Round 1	5	5	4	5	4	4	4	3	3	4	3	4	4	4	5	5	6	4	76
Scotland	**T100**	Round 2	4	4	4	4	4	4	4	3	5	4	3	4	4	5	4	4	4	4	72 -**148**
Brian Davis	T128	Round 1	6	5	4	4	6	4	3	3	4	4	3	3	5	5	4	5	6	3	77
England	**T100**	Round 2	5	4	4	3	5	4	4	3	3	4	3	4	4	5	4	4	5	3	71 -**148**
Charl Schwartzel	T116	Round 1	4	5	3	4	5	3	4	3	4	4	3	4	4	7	5	5	5	4	76
South Africa	**T100**	Round 2	4	4	4	4	5	4	4	2	3	4	3	4	4	5	5	4	5	4	72 -**148**
Ignacio Garrido	T30	Round 1	4	4	4	4	4	3	5	3	3	5	3	4	4	6	4	4	4	3	71
Spain	**T100**	Round 2	4	5	4	4	4	6	4	4	3	4	4	4	6	4	4	4	5	4	77 -**148**
Scott Hend	T56	Round 1	3	7	5	3	4	4	3	3	3	5	4	3	4	4	5	4	5	4	73
Australia	**T114**	Round 2	4	4	4	4	4	4	4	4	4	5	4	4	5	5	5	4	4	4	76 -**149**
Shigeki Maruyama	T128	Round 1	6	3	4	5	5	4	4	3	5	3	5	3	6	4	6	4	5	4	77
Japan	**T114**	Round 2	4	4	4	4	4	4	3	3	3	4	4	5	4	5	4	5	4		72 -**149**
Kenneth Ferrie	T74	Round 1	4	5	4	4	5	4	3	3	3	4	4	4	5	4	4	5	5	4	74
England	**T114**	Round 2	4	4	4	5	5	4	4	3	6	4	3	4	5	4	4	5	4	3	75 -**149**
Martin Doyle	T56	Round 1	4	4	3	5	6	3	4	4	3	4	3	5	5	4	4	4	4	4	73
Australia	**T114**	Round 2	4	5	4	4	5	4	5	3	4	3	3	3	5	5	4	4	7	4	76 -**149**
Stewart Cink	T116	Round 1	4	5	4	4	5	4	4	4	4	4	3	4	5	6	4	4	4	4	76
USA	**T114**	Round 2	4	5	4	4	5	5	4	3	2	4	3	5	3	6	4	4	5	3	73 -**149**
Davis Love III	T98	Round 1	3	4	4	5	5	4	4	4	4	5	4	4	6	5	4	3	4	3	75
USA	**T114**	Round 2	3	4	4	5	4	5	4	3	5	4	3	4	4	7	4	4	4	3	74 -**149**
Angel Cabrera	T98	Round 1	4	4	4	5	5	3	5	3	3	4	4	4	5	5	3	4	6	4	75
Argentina	**T114**	Round 2	4	4	4	4	4	5	4	4	4	5	3	3	5	4	5	4	5	3	74 -**149**
David Diaz	T74	Round 1	4	4	4	4	5	4	5	3	4	5	4	4	4	5	4	4	4	3	74
Australia	**T114**	Round 2	4	4	4	4	4	5	3	3	3	4	4	4	6	5	4	4	5	5	75 -**149**
Lars Brovold	T98	Round 1	5	4	4	3	5	4	4	4	4	5	3	4	4	5	4	4	6	3	75
Norway	**T114**	Round 2	4	5	5	4	4	5	4	3	3	4	3	4	5	5	4	4	4	4	74 -**149**
Paul Casey	T98	Round 1	4	5	4	5	5	4	4	4	3	4	3	5	4	5	4	4	5	3	75
England	**T123**	Round 2	5	4	4	4	4	4	3	3	3	4	5	5	5	5	5	5	5	3	75 -**150**
Jean Van de Velde	T128	Round 1	4	5	4	5	5	5	3	3	4	4	3	5	5	4	4	4	6	4	77
France	**T123**	Round 2	4	4	4	4	5	5	4	3	4	4	3	4	4	4	4	4	5	4	73 -**150**

HOLE			1	2	3	4	5	6	7	8	9	10	11	12	13	14	15	16	17	18	
PAR	POSITION		4	4	4	4	5	4	4	3	4	4	3	4	4	5	4	4	4	4	TOTAL
Robert Coles	T116	Round 1	5	4	4	6	5	4	5	3	4	4	3	4	4	5	5	3	4	4	76
England	**T123**	Round 2	4	5	4	4	5	3	3	3	5	4	4	3	5	5	4	4	5	4	74 -**150**
Stephen Ames	T116	Round 1	5	5	4	4	5	4	4	3	4	3	3	5	4	4	5	4	7	3	76
Canada	**T123**	Round 2	4	4	4	4	4	4	4	2	3	4	3	5	4	5	5	5	5	5	74 -**150**
Douglas McGuigan	T74	Round 1	4	4	4	4	5	4	4	4	3	5	3	4	4	5	4	5	5	4	74
Scotland	**T123**	Round 2	4	5	4	5	4	4	4	3	4	4	3	4	4	6	5	4	5	4	76 -**150**
Chad Campbell	T138	Round 1	4	7	4	4	4	4	5	4	4	5	3	5	5	4	4	4	4	4	78
USA	**T128**	Round 2	6	4	4	4	5	4	4	3	3	4	3	3	4	5	4	4	5	4	73 -**151**
Mike Weir	T116	Round 1	4	4	5	5	6	4	4	4	4	4	3	4	4	4	4	4	5	4	76
Canada	**T128**	Round 2	4	5	4	4	5	5	4	4	3	4	3	4	5	4	5	4	5	3	75 -**151**
Rich Barcelo	T149	Round 1	5	5	4	5	5	4	4	4	4	3	4	4	4	5	5	4	7	4	80
USA	**T128**	Round 2	4	3	3	4	4	4	3	3	4	4	3	4	4	4	4	7	5	4	71 -**151**
Rory Sabbatini	T41	Round 1	4	5	4	5	4	4	4	2	3	4	4	4	4	6	4	4	4	3	72
South Africa	**T128**	Round 2	4	4	4	5	6	5	4	3	4	4	3	4	5	5	4	6	5	4	79 -**151**
***Oscar Floren**	T56	Round 1	4	5	4	4	4	3	4	4	4	4	3	4	4	6	4	4	5	3	73
Sweden	**T128**	Round 2	5	4	4	4	5	4	4	3	4	4	3	4	4	6	5	6	7	3	78 -**151**
Murray Urquhart	T56	Round 1	4	4	5	4	5	3	4	4	4	4	4	4	4	4	4	5	4	3	73
Scotland	**T128**	Round 2	5	4	4	5	6	5	4	3	3	5	3	3	4	5	4	6	5	4	78 -**151**
Andre Bossert	T74	Round 1	4	4	3	4	6	4	4	3	4	4	4	4	4	6	4	4	4	4	74
Switzerland	**T128**	Round 2	4	5	3	5	6	4	4	4	5	4	4	4	5	4	4	4	4	4	77 -**151**
Tim Petrovic	T128	Round 1	5	5	4	3	6	4	4	3	4	4	3	4	4	6	5	4	5	4	77
USA	**T135**	Round 2	3	5	4	5	6	4	4	3	4	4	3	4	4	6	3	4	5	4	75 -**152**
Peter Lawrie	T74	Round 1	4	4	4	4	4	4	4	4	4	3	4	4	6	4	4	4	5	4	74
Ireland	**T135**	Round 2	4	5	4	4	5	5	4	3	5	4	4	5	5	5	4	5	5	3	78 -**152**
Craig Parry	T138	Round 1	4	5	4	5	6	4	4	3	4	4	3	5	4	6	4	4	4	5	78
Australia	**T135**	Round 2	4	5	4	5	4	5	4	3	3	4	3	3	5	5	4	4	5	4	74 -**152**
Wilhelm Schauman	T151	Round 1	4	5	4	4	6	5	3	3	4	4	5	6	5	5	4	6	5	3	81
Sweden	**T135**	Round 2	3	4	5	4	4	4	4	4	3	4	3	3	5	4	4	4	5	4	71 -**152**
***Robert Steele**	T138	Round 1	4	5	3	5	5	5	4	3	4	4	4	4	6	7	4	4	3	4	78
England	**T139**	Round 2	4	6	4	4	4	4	4	3	5	4	3	4	4	5	4	4	5	4	75 -**153**
Sean McDonagh	T128	Round 1	4	5	3	4	5	4	4	4	5	4	3	5	4	5	5	5	4	4	77
England	**T139**	Round 2	5	6	4	3	6	4	4	3	3	4	3	4	4	5	5	4	5	4	76 -**153**
Marcus Fraser	T138	Round 1	4	5	3	6	5	5	5	3	3	5	3	4	4	5	5	4	5	4	78
Australia	**T139**	Round 2	4	5	4	5	6	4	4	3	4	3	3	3	5	5	5	4	5	3	75 -**153**
Rich Beem	T74	Round 1	3	4	4	4	5	5	5	2	5	4	3	4	4	6	4	4	4	4	74
USA	**T139**	Round 2	4	4	5	5	6	4	4	3	4	4	4	4	5	6	4	4	5	4	79 -**153**
***Brian McElhinney**	T138	Round 1	4	5	3	4	6	5	4	3	4	4	3	5	5	5	6	4	4	4	78
Ireland	**T139**	Round 2	4	4	4	6	5	3	3	3	4	4	3	4	5	7	3	4	5	4	75 -**153**
Toru Taniguchi	T98	Round 1	4	4	4	4	5	4	5	3	4	4	3	4	6	5	4	4	5	3	75
Japan	**T139**	Round 2	4	4	4	3	7	4	5	3	4	4	2	3	6	6	4	5	7	3	78 -**153**
Stephen Gallacher	T98	Round 1	4	4	3	4	4	4	4	3	4	5	3	4	4	4	5	4	6	6	75
Scotland	**T139**	Round 2	5	4	5	4	4	4	4	2	3	4	4	8	5	4	5	4	5	4	78 -**153**
Andrew Butterfield	T128	Round 1	3	5	4	5	5	3	4	3	4	4	3	4	6	5	4	5	6	4	77
England	**T139**	Round 2	5	4	4	4	4	5	4	3	4	4	4	5	4	5	5	5	4	3	76 -**153**
Chris Campbell	T151	Round 1	4	5	4	4	5	5	6	4	5	5	3	5	5	4	4	5	4	4	81
Australia	**T147**	Round 2	5	4	4	4	3	4	4	3	3	4	3	4	5	5	4	4	7	4	74 -**155**

HOLE			1	2	3	4	5	6	7	8	9	10	11	12	13	14	15	16	17	18	
PAR	POSITION		4	4	4	4	5	4	4	3	4	4	3	4	4	5	4	4	4	4	TOTAL
Tony Jacklin	T146	Round 1	4	7	4	4	4	4	4	3	3	4	3	4	4	8	6	4	5	4	79
England	**T147**	Round 2	3	4	3	4	5	4	4	3	4	4	4	4	5	7	4	4	6	4	76 -**155**
David Duval	T149	Round 1	4	4	5	4	4	4	4	4	4	4	4	4	5	6	6	4	6	4	80
USA	**T149**	Round 2	4	5	3	5	5	4	4	3	3	4	4	5	4	7	4	3	6	4	77 -**157**
Tom Pernice	T138	Round 1	4	8	4	4	4	5	4	4	3	5	4	4	4	6	4	5	3	3	78
USA	**T149**	Round 2	4	3	4	6	4	4	4	3	3	4	3	7	4	9	4	5	4	4	79 -**157**
John Wade	T116	Round 1	5	4	4	5	7	5	4	3	3	4	3	4	5	4	4	4	5	3	76
Australia	**T151**	Round 2	4	5	4	5	6	5	6	3	3	4	5	3	5	5	5	5	5	4	82 -**158**
Andrew Marshall	T155	Round 1	4	6	5	5	7	5	4	3	3	4	5	4	4	6	5	5	5	4	84
England	**T151**	Round 2	3	5	5	4	4	5	4	4	3	4	3	4	4	5	4	4	5	4	74 -**158**
Richard Moir	154	Round 1	4	5	4	4	8	4	4	4	4	4	3	6	4	5	5	5	7	3	83
Australia	**T151**	Round 2	4	5	4	4	4	5	3	3	5	6	4	3	4	6	4	3	4	4	75 -**158**
Peter Oakley	T151	Round 1	4	4	4	5	5	4	6	3	4	5	2	5	5	6	7	3	5	4	81
USA	**154**	Round 2	4	4	5	5	5	4	4	4	4	4	3	4	5	4	4	6	5	4	78 -**159**
Thammanoon Srirot	T155	Round 1	4	5	4	6	7	5	4	3	5	5	4	4	4	4	5	4	7	4	84
Thailand	**155**	Round 2	3	4	4	7	5	4	6	3	4	4	3	4	5	5	4	5	4	3	77 -**161**
David Toms	156	Round 1	4	4	3	4	4	4	4	4	3	3	4	4	6	4	5	4	6	4	74 -**DQ**
USA																					

PHOTOGRAPHY CREDITS
(All © Getty Images)

David Cannon – front and back covers, 8-9, 10, 12, 13, 14, 16, 19, 35 bottom, 39 bottom, 42, 44, 49 bottom, 55, 74, 90, 95, 99, 101, 103, 107 top, 109 middle, 110 middle, 113, 127

Stanley Chou – 20 top left

Scott Halleran – 20 top right

Richard Heathcote – 21 right, 26, 29 bottom, 30 top right, 30 bottom, 32, 41, 46 right, 50 left (2), 52 right, 56 top, 64, 68, 70, 75 bottom left, 76 top left, top middle, 77, 86 left, 87 top, 88 top right, 89, 94 right, 98, 100, 106 top, 109 left, 115 second from right

Ross Kinnaird – 6, 35 top, 36, 57, 59, 66 (2), 69 right, 72 bottom, 75 top, 82, 104, 106-107 bottom, 109 right, 114 bottom left, 115 second from left

Warren Little – 21 left, 45, 47 bottom, 54 right, 61 bottom, 63, 71, 73, 83, 84, 88 bottom, 96, 115 right, 116

Chris McGrath – 20 bottom

Steve Powell – 49 top

Andrew Redington – 24, 27, 28, 31, 34, 39 top, 40 top, 52 left (2), 53, 54 left, 54 middle, 61 top (3), 76 top right, bottom, 80, 86 right, 88 top left, 91 left, 92, 94 left, 97 top, 110 right, 111 (3), 112, 114 top

Jamie Squire – 22, 25, 29 top, 30 top left, 33, 37, 38, 40 bottom, 46 left, 47 top (2), 48, 50 top right, 56 bottom, 58, 60, 69 left, 72 top (2), 75 bottom right, 78, 81, 87 bottom, 91 right, 97 bottom, 105, 110 left, 114 bottom right, 115 left

THE OLD COURSE
ST ANDREWS